Endorsements

"As someone who cares deeply about mental health, *Us In Mind* was such a refreshing read on how to incorporate neurological science into our most important relationship. Ted offers practical steps all of us can take to not just invest in our marriage, but also invest in our own mental and spiritual well-being. We will all be better off for having read this book!"

—Chinwé Williams, PhD

"I love this book! I knew I would because I have deep respect and admiration for Ted Lowe. Ted is one of the key leaders in the marriage ministry movement around the world. He is practical and authentic just like this book. Every chapter encouraged and motivated me to create a more intimate marriage."

—Jim Burns, PhD
President, HomeWord
Author of *Doing Life With Adult Children: Keep Your Mouth Shut and the Welcome Mat Out* and *Creating an Intimate Marriage*

"Ted's passion for marriages is evident in the quality of information he shares and his unique way of sharing ideas that married couples can easily implement. This book is an amazing resource for me and our marriage team."

—Linda Vujnov, Marriage Pastor, Mariners Church, Irvine, CA

"This book is going to be a game changer for marriages. Plus, one of the things I always love about Ted's work is his ability to make people think while never forgetting to make them laugh. *Us In Mind* is surely no exception."

—Julie Baumgardner
Senior Director of WinShape Marriage

"For 20 years I've watched up close as Ted has helped countless couples love each other better. But the real reason you should read this book is because for 20 years I've watched up close as Ted has loved Nancie. When Ted writes or speaks, I listen. Not because of his accomplishments, but because he is the real deal. I want to have a marriage like his and Nancie's."

—John McGee
Director of Resources, Watermark Church

"Ted Lowe uses humor, personal stories, and Scripture that all work to equip you to change your marriage by changing your mind. We consider this book to be an invaluable resource for those (like us) who are committed to making their marriage a masterpiece. Together we are reading, studying, laughing, applying what Ted said, and sharing what we have learned from this book with others."

—Montell and Kristin Jordan
Recording Artists and Lead Pastors of Master Peace Church/ Marriage Masterpeace Retreat Center, Grammy nominated singer-songwriter, #1 recording artist

"Ted Lowe's new book has so many nuggets of wisdom in it. I want to purchase a copy for every newlywed couple I know...and some grumpy old married couples as well! The way we think about our spouses and the intent we assign to their behavior is a game changer to viewing your lifetime partner in an empathetic way. Ted weaves great stories, research, and encouraging spiritual wisdom into one great book."

—Jána Guynn
Director of Marrieds, Gwinnett Church

"Ted Lowe has a unique gift to communicate deep truths in a totally understandable and relatable way. In *Us In Mind* he offers solid biblical and research backed principles to make your marriage better. And guess what...you'll actually have fun reading this book."

—Mathew Turvey, Psy.D.
Chick-fil-A, Inc.

"In *Us In Mind*, Ted shows that having a happy marriage involves not only what we do but also what we think. Ted's passion to see couples thrive is evident throughout the stories he shares and practical advice he provides. As I read this book, it felt as if a trusted friend pulled up a chair to offer his experience and encouragement to make my marriage the best it can be."

—Steve Giddens
Director of Digital Content, North Point Church, Atlanta, GA

"As someone who struggles with his thoughts, I immediately knew *Us In Mind* would benefit me individually and in my marriage. Ted shares personal stories, biblical wisdom, and decades of marriage ministry experience as he helps us understand how our thought life directly impacts our marriage."

—Scott Kedersha
Marriage Pastor, Harris Creek Baptist Church, Author of *Ready or Knot? 12 Conversations Every Couple Needs to Have before Marriage*

"The first time Ted did his event at our church, the #1 thing that resonated with me was: Our thoughts matter the most in our marriages. After reading the book, I have to say I'm so excited about this book and even more excited for the couples who'll read it! *Us In Mind* will be a staple for our marriage and a staple when we coach and mentor other couples!"

—Jackie and Stephana Bledsoe
Bestselling authors, speakers, and co-founders of HappilyMarriedCouples.com

Us in Mind: How Changing Your Thoughts Can Change Your Marriage
Published by Orange, a division of The reThink Group, Inc.
5870 Charlotte Lane, Suite 300
Cumming, GA 30040 U.S.A.

ISBN: 978-1-63570-196-8

Author: Ted Lowe
Editor: Sarah Anderson
Cover Design: Ashley Shugart
Interior Design: Ashley Shugart, Anna Kay Miller
Executive Director of Publishing: Mike Jeffries
Project Manager: Brian Sharp
Director of Publishing Marketing: Brandon Carter

Printed in the United States of America
First Edition 2022

1 2 3 4 5 6 7 8 9 10

08/31/2022

HOW CHANGING YOUR THOUGHTS
CAN CHANGE YOUR MARRIAGE

Us In Mind

by Ted Lowe

orange

Dedication

To My Kibbutz,

For the better part of a decade, it has been one of my greatest joys and my marriage's greatest assets to do life with all of you, our self-titled Kibbutz. I love that your marriages are the ones that surround ours. It's staggering to think of the sum total of gains and losses we have shared together. There is no group on the earth I would rather share them with. You bring so much life to my life.

So, I dedicate this book to all of you primarily and selfishly because you would love and support me if I never wrote another word. In fact, most of you won't even read this book, and that is the very reason I'm dedicating it to you! (Kevin, I applaud you if you can get through this entire paragraph.) You all love me for me, and I love all of you for you; which is important for an Enneagram 3.

So, it is with great joy I dedicate this book to:

- Kim and Kevin Neel
- Shelly and Pat Malone
- Jen and Casey Myers
- Lynn and Greg Payne

Thanks for your encouragement through the writing of this book, but mostly, the living of this life.

Whenever you are ready, I'm ready to sell it all and build our own literal Kibbutz,

Ted

Acknowledgments

To my Pug,
Oh, my love, your wisdom, love, laughter, and encouragement are on every page of this book. You have allowed me to share our marriage in a vulnerable and transparent way. You have supported and encouraged me to write despite all the things about me that make it difficult. You are my best friend, my person, the other half of my Us. You make everything matter more. "I love you real good!"

To Sarah Anderson,
When I heard you agreed to be my editor, I was thrilled. I knew your brilliance as an author, combined with your heart for EVERY human on the planet, would make this a much better book. That has certainly turned out to be the case! Thank you for the countless hours you invested. Because of you, more people will feel loved and encouraged by the pages of this book.

To Shelly Malone,
Thank you for being the person in our Kibbutz who said, "I would love to find typos in your book." I took that for what it was and not a slam. Thanks for partnering with me during the early stages when I was writing this all alone. Your encouragement and finding of errors mattered to me and to this book.

To Dr. Jerome, Steve Giddens, Todd Graham, Jana Guynn, Scott Kedersha, Greg Payne, Dr. Josh Straub, Dr. Matt Turvey, and Linda Vujnov, I sent you this book while it was still malleable. I wanted you to have it before it became too finalized so your hearts and heads could make it better. You all did that in big and small ways. I am beyond grateful.

Foreword

What does it look like to pursue health? To become the healthiest version of ourselves inside this thing we call marriage?

As someone who has been married for 17 years and has three children, I've asked that question of myself a lot. And when it comes to marriage, I am constantly trying to navigate the spectrum of what it means sometimes to survive, thrive, and everything in between.

That's why I so appreciate this book. Friends, I can tell you without any hesitation, what you're holding is exactly what we need.

Us In Mind not only offers contemporary brain science, but a way to navigate relationships through practical applications as well as the spiritual context for how our brains and our bodies are showing up in certain situations. Throughout his book, Ted directs us towards this thing called neuroplasticity, of our capacity for real and tangible change that begins with something as simple as intentionality.

Ted reminds us that choosing intentionality is something all of us can do. We don't have to be a natural at marriage, we just need to commit to working towards being better, remembering practice doesn't make perfect... practice makes permanent. So, the question for all of us in marriage becomes, "What are we practicing?" *Us In Mind* offers us novel and scientifically proven ways to practice habits that will make us better spouses and better people.

Ted does that in *Us In Mind* by giving us five intentional thoughts we can begin to incorporate into our day-to-day lives right now. He does so with compassion and humor, patiently encouraging us to practice more self-awareness by examining our own habits before passing judgment on our spouses.

I couldn't be more behind what Ted offers in this book. (Except when it comes to his dishwashing team. We'll have to agree to disagree on that one.)

Ultimately, what Ted shows us is that marriage oftentimes is not simply about coexisting. It's about coalescing—blending, integrating, merging, becoming one... for better, or for worse, in order to cultivate a healthy relationship inside ourselves, with our spouse, and with the God who made us and loves us.

More than anything, by the time you finish this book, you will find Ted left you with a tool box that will help you better engage with your spouse resulting in healthy connection, healthy vulnerability, and healthy sacrifice. I couldn't love what Ted has said more. *Us In Mind* will do more than just give you a kick start to your marriage, it will show Ted as he really is—a cheerleader and champion of marriage, who wants the best for you and your spouse and not just a way to stick a marriage out. Ted wants your marriage to win, and *Us In Mind* provides the game plan to do just that.

—Dr. Jerome D. Lubbe, Functional Neurologist, author *The Brain-Based Enneagram: You Are Not A Number*, CEO & Founder of Thrive Neuro Health

Table of Contents

Chapter One

What Do You Think It Takes to Have A Great Marriage?

IN 2001, AFTER SIX YEARS OF MARRIAGE, I got an opportunity I still can't believe was possible. After being in youth ministry since 1993, I was offered the job of Director of Married Life at a large church in an Atlanta suburb. I said yes. And with that "yes," my full-time job and full-time ministry became marriage. On paper then, and maybe even now, it didn't make sense. I had little experience in this ministry area. I had only been married six years myself. I was not a marriage expert—by a long shot. But I was eager and enthusiastic, and I was hoping that would count for something.

From my years working in youth ministry, I had seen firsthand the ripple effect marriage has on families and communities. I had learned that marriage—and you know this—doesn't just impact the couple. There are countless people in the wake of every marriage, so to be able to invest in marriages, that would in turn positively impact the next generation, seemed like an ideal scenario. In addition, there was the fact that my wife Nancie and I had been fortunate enough to be surrounded by great marriages from the first day of our own marriage. We had seen that marriage should and could be great, and to be able to encourage others like we had been encouraged seemed like an incredible opportunity.

But maybe most of all, I was excited for this chance because over our short marriage, we had learned a few simple marital habits that had changed us and the way we saw our marriage and each other. I saw this new job as an opportunity to share those habits with as many people as possible. They were simple principles, and we were proof that they worked.

With this change in direction from youth ministry to marriage ministry, I remember thinking to myself, "I'm going to make this job count. I'm going to learn everything there is about marriage." So, I went to the place everyone went in 2001 to learn everything there is about marriage: Barnes and Noble. I will never forget how overwhelmed I felt as I stood before the marriage section. There must have been at least 100 different titles full of philosophies and advice, ranging from simplistic
to scientific.

It was a lot.

And all I could think was: Which of these titles hold the truth? There were so many ideas and so many formulas and promises and tips and quizzes and it was enough to melt my ADHD brain. Then something hit me in the chest that hasn't left me since. I thought about the people who were married but their full-time jobs weren't to focus on marriage—you know, almost every married person on the planet. I thought about people walking up to the same mountain of content I was witnessing, feeling completely overwhelmed, and walking away more discouraged than ever by the mass of resources and lack of clarity.

As a result of that day, I vowed, to the best of my ability, to research and find what makes marriage great. I wanted to give married people "go and do's" they could actually *go and do*. I wanted to help marriages in more practical, fun, and simple ways. And that's what I've been attempting to do ever since—through speaking, writing, and creating resources.

The truth is, I feel like marriage is *my thing*. And listen, I get it. When people hear me say helping marriage is what I feel like God has called me to do, it can sound strange. Especially because there are a lot of sad marital stats and stories. In fact, you may have experienced one growing up or are experiencing one now. But despite the state of some marriages, I know a better marriage is possible for most. That's why I keep going; because I want you to know there are also countless stories of couples who change their minds and their habits and it changes their marriage. I have seen it in my own marriage and witnessed it in others. And when someone tells me after an event, "Now that made sense. I can do that", I think to myself, *That's why I do this*. It keeps me in the game.

Also, if I'm being really honest, one of the things I *love* most about investing in marriages is that it gives me the opportunity to make couples laugh. And when it comes to marriage, laughing is a big deal. It matters. If you've been married for any amount of time you know: marriage is a funny, funny thing. And I love watching married couples laugh and elbow each other when they relate to what I'm communicating. When I put all of that together, it adds up to me having more hope and energy for marriage now than I did in 2001 when I started my career in the marriage world. And hope, in today's world, in any capacity, is something we could all use more of.

So, What Are We Doing Here?

Despite my enthusiasm and optimism for all marriages, over the past few decades, there were some consistent issues couples were facing that kept popping up. And no matter what I did, I just couldn't figure them out—until a few years ago.

Mystery #1: Why do some married people respond to marriage advice while others don't?

I didn't understand...

- Why some couples read a marriage book, apply what they read, and it changes their lives...while others get nothing from the same book.

- Why some couples come to a marriage event and apply principles from Scripture and research...while others write it off as ill-advised or impossible.
- Why some couples meet with me, ask for my advice, and then take it...while others meet with me, never ask a single question, and spend the whole time debating over the details of their last fight.

Mystery #2: Why would someone get a divorce without first seeking help?

Perhaps the most mystifying and devastating thing for me is when I get the news about family members and friends who have gotten or are getting a divorce without first seeking counsel. People research everything—from Bitcoin to how to remove a grease stain—but when it comes to marriage, too many people don't go looking for help at all.

On some level, I get it. Marriage is my life—it's my actual job—so of course I think it should be of utmost importance to everyone. I'm sure financial advisors and personal trainers are also baffled why people aren't more fiscally and physically responsible. Nonetheless, with so much at stake, why do married people not try everything possible before calling it quits?

Mystery #3: What makes some couples thrive, some couples quit, and others just survive?

Why is it that some couples experience tremendous stress, even tragedy, and remain hopeful in who they are? Why do chaos, circumstances, and the everyday stress of life in general seem to draw some closer, while pushing others apart?

Searching for Clues

These mysteries have circled my brain for years. So I finally decided to try to solve these mysteries for myself. I did a deep dive. When I did, what I discovered convinced me I needed to write this book.

And let me tell you, I *needed* convincing. I didn't want to write another book. I'd already written two and neither was a walk in the park—unless a walk in the park includes months of torture. If that's the case, writing a book is exactly like a walk in the park. I didn't want to go through that again. PLUS: I've had ADHD since long before it was cool to have it. For me, writing a book is like lassoing squirrels and then training them not to fidget.

But despite the mental wrangling I knew this book would require, I couldn't ignore the nagging feeling that it was something I had to do. I felt I *had* to write it because most people don't know what I'm going to share with you, and the power of knowing it, followed by some simple applications, can be utterly transformational.

ADHD SIDE-SQUIRREL ALERT: Writing this book is even worth the pain I'm experiencing at this very moment. I needed a fresh place to write, so right now, I'm trying out the public library. I'm at a desk, my ears filled with an ocean waves soundtrack as I desperately try to drown out a lady passionately doing something with papers and a stapler. Unfortunately, my $3 airplane earphones are worth no dollars, and her stapler has surround sound.

But YOU are worth the madness my ADHD makes me feel. Because I can say to you with integrity: I care about your marriage. I want your marriage to win. I'm for you. I'm for your spouse. I believe what you are going to learn has great power. I think it might even be appropriate for you to get a little giddy considering what might happen to your relationship—to your *Us*.

Imagine less conflict and more connection. Imagine more laughter and less fighting. Imagine being able to model something you hope your kids inherit in their own relationships. Doesn't that sound good? *It is.* But I'm getting ahead of myself.

The discoveries I made started with me asking this question: **What does it take to have a *great* marriage?** Not a so-so marriage—a great one.

When I started with that question, I discovered more than I could have ever bargained for, including why some people are receptive to marriage enrichment and others aren't, and why some couples thrive and others don't. The mysteries all seemed to revolve around one thing: what makes a marriage great.

So, how do we get to great when it comes to our own marriage?

What I discovered and what we are going to discover in this book, is that research and Scripture have had something to say to us about this all along. Are you ready for this?

When it comes to your marriage, your thoughts matter most.

Your *thinking* matters most. *And thinking is the thing most of us aren't thinking about.* Most of us are just along for the mental ride, be it good, bad, or ugly. We aren't actively doing anything to direct our thoughts or change our thoughts. We simply think them. And while that may not sound like a big deal, it is. Because the way we think radically impacts... *everything*. Let me explain.

What If a Great Marriage Isn't the Opposite of a Struggling One?

For years, researchers didn't study great marriages. They studied *stuck* and *struggling* marriages with the hopes of helping couples avoid the hurdles or habits that lead to an unhappy partnership. These social scientists believed that by better understanding struggling marriages, they could help couples develop great ones. Makes sense.

Here's what they found. They discovered that in unhappy marriages, spouses didn't understand each other. Additionally, unhappy couples couldn't accurately identify each other's strengths and weaknesses. So, counselors worked to help couples have a clearer understanding of who their spouse TRULY was.

But even when counselors helped spouses better understand each other, it often didn't help improve the marriages. So, a group of leading researchers from the School of Positive Psychology took a different approach. They argued that if we want to know the distinct characteristics of great marriages, **we must study great marriages with the same intensity that has been given to studying ones that were struggling.** In other words, they wanted to figure out what makes a great marriage, great.

What they discovered blew me away at first, but now makes perfect sense. It turns out, their hunch was right. Just like great business owners, great athletes, and great parents aren't simply the opposite of struggling ones, it turns out great marriages are NOT just the opposite of struggling marriages.

They are different in a very specific way.

For instance, in one study conducted by Dr. Sandra Murray and her colleagues from The State University of New York,[1] couples were given a list of qualities and asked to rate their spouse on them. These qualities included things like: (1) "kind and affectionate," (2) "open and disclosing," (3) "patient," (4) "warm," (5) "sociable", etc.

Now, if we were to stick to the original premise—that good marriages understand each other—then it would seem that when a husband rates his wife high on "patience" and low on "sociable" and his wife ranks herself the same way—meaning they're in sync—they should be a very happy couple. But the research proved this wasn't true at all!

The study discovered one distinct pattern that emerged in the happiest of couples. **The happiest, most satisfied couples were the ones where one person rated their partner more positively than their partner rated themselves...*in every single category*.**

Turns out, an accurate understanding of each other's strengths and weaknesses does not make us more satisfied in marriage. Or, to put it another way, mutual understanding doesn't make a happy marriage.

The people who saw their partner *as better than they saw themselves*—or, love-blind couples—were happiest. In other words, a happy marriage was made up of two people who **thought** of one another, *"I wish you could see you the way I see you."* They were seeing their spouse through rose-colored glasses.

Now, you might be thinking—like I was—*"There's no way love blindness can last, right?"* The researchers wondered the same thing and tracked these couples to see what would happen if spouses did not live up to the high view their spouse had of them. When the couples discovered their spouse wasn't as great as they imagined, surely marital satisfaction would plummet, right? Actually, *no*. These couples were not only *more* satisfied with the relationship later, they also reported fewer sources of conflict and fewer moments of doubt. So, there you have it. **Spouses**

who think highly of each other have a strong marriage today, and an even stronger one tomorrow.

What Are They Thinking?

The same findings have proven true from a neurological perspective. Dr. Helen Fisher, a renowned biological anthropologist, conducted a brain-scan study of people who had been married an average of 21 years who reported they are still madly in love.[2] They all showed similar activity in three brain regions—all of which we will briefly look at in this book. But for now, we'll focus on just one. These still-madly-in-love couples had a high level of activity in the area of the brain responsible for positive illusions.

Positive illusions are defined as the simple—but sometimes challenging—**ability to overlook what you don't like about somebody in order to focus on what you do like**. In other words, this study affirms, again, **your thoughts matter most to your marriage**.

For happily married people, their thoughts guide them towards having the marriage they hope for. Whether they are born that way or whether they learned it, their mindsets are set to think well of their spouse. And thinking highly of their spouse ultimately affects behavior toward their spouse. A highly thought of spouse is a well-loved spouse.

For you, this may be great news. This is just scientific evidence of why you are crushing it. But for many of us, finding out that our thoughts matter most to our marriage doesn't seem like good news. Some of us aren't having good thoughts about ourselves, our spouse, and ultimately our marriage. We aren't deliberately choosing negative thoughts, but they often show up regularly and without invitation. As a result, **many of our automatic thoughts aren't automatically good for our marriage**.

Maybe you think things like:

- "Why should *I* try? My spouse never tries."
- "Experts? Yeah, right. What do they know?"
- "I'm not the one who needs to change. She needs to change."
- "I'm just not attracted to him."
- "I deserve to be happy."
- "Divorce is not uncommon. It's the right option for us."

— "Marriage is an outdated institution. Who needs it?"
— "This is my truth. I want to live my truth."
— "You just don't know my story."

If your thoughts are negative, you are not alone. According to the National Science Foundation, people on average have about 12,000 to 60,000 thoughts per day. Eighty percent of those thoughts are negative and 95% are repetitive. That being said, no matter what category we fall into when it comes to our thinking patterns—positive or negative—we all need to consider our thinking. These automatic thoughts have an innate ability to shape our attitudes and actions which makes them infinitely more powerful than we give them credit for. So while **your automatic thoughts aren't your attitudes or actions, they are the catalyst for both**.

Give Me Some Hope

But here's the great news for all of us, and the heart of this book. You don't have to let your thoughts run on auto-pilot. You don't have to become a victim to thinking that leads to actions that push your spouse away. You have more control of your thoughts than perhaps you have been led to believe or ever dreamed possible.

A lot of us never question our thoughts because they've always been with us. Plus, most of us were never taught in school or church to think about what we think about. The only thing I heard in church about my thoughts was to make sure I kept them pure—sexually. And while that's important, that's nowhere near the full story of what our thoughts can and can't do for us. I was never taught I had any real power over my thoughts. But I do. *You* do. We do not have to become victims to the automatic nature of our thoughts!

In fact, **one of the best things you could do for your marriage is learn how to change your mind**. Not change your spouse, but change your *mind*. That's what has benefited me and my marriage to Nancie more than I could have imagined. It's been a game changer for us and it's made me determined to share what we have experienced with as many people as possible. Even if that means enduring my own personal mental Cirque Du Soleil of writing another book.

But before we move forward. I want to pause here and say if you are suffering from (1) abuse, (2) infidelity, or (3) harmful situations, this book isn't enough for you right now. If you are experiencing any of these situations, I'm truly so sorry. I've spoken with people who are hurting in the same ways and the pain these circumstances cause can be unbearable. While the previously mentioned situations are beyond the scope of this book, you are not—and you should not—be alone. You need to close this book and get some help from a friend, family member, pastor, or counselor...now. Please take this moment as a prompt not to wait any longer to get safe and find the support you need.

For most couples however, what we are exploring in this book *is* right for you, even if it sounds like an impossible task. It is designed to help you think about how you're thinking because *if we can change our minds, we can change our marriage*. Knowing we are able to shift our mindset could be the hope you need to imagine a better future for your marriage.

But How Do We Start to Change Our Minds?

When I discovered the studies on the importance of, and ability to, change our thoughts, I was thrilled. In fact, I drove my family, friends, and co-workers a little crazy talking about it. I couldn't keep this information to myself. As a pastor and follower of Jesus, I was thrilled once again to see how research aligns with Scripture. I've seen marriages be transformed when mindsets are changed. Romans 12:2 puts it this way:

> *Do not conform to the pattern of this world, but be transformed by the renewing of your mind. Then you will be able to test and approve what God's will is—his good, pleasing and perfect will (NIV).*

There it is. In plain sight. *We can be transformed by renewing our mind.* I'm not sure how I missed it for so long! I went to seminary, I've heard thousands of sermons, read tons of books, but somehow, I missed the huge emphasis God places on not allowing our thoughts to run on auto-pilot.

In fact, I love those two words Paul uses in this letter to the Romans: **test** and **approve**. We can test and approve what we are thinking. In Greek, those two words are actually a phrase that mean we can discern, we can examine, we can be thoughtful about our thoughts. We can be wise about what we are thinking. And when we do that, it helps us to live out God's good, pleasing, and perfect will.

2 Corinthians 10:5 talks about this same idea in a different way using the words: *demolish and take captive*:

> *We **demolish** arguments and every pretension that sets itself up against the knowledge of God, and we **take captive** every thought to make it obedient to Christ (NIV).*

Paul is referring to the idea of us taking our thoughts captive, grabbing them from our minds, and saying, "Hold on a minute, is this thought taking me where I want to go?" When we test, approve, demolish, and take captive our thoughts, things change—including our marriage.

And this isn't just a sales pitch. I've seen marriages, including my own marriage, be transformed by the renewing of the mind. How? **By allowing Scripture to reset your mind, you can reset your marriage.**

Even if you aren't sure how you feel about the Bible, God, or Jesus directing your marriage, there's no denying that the research and neuroscience come to the same conclusions. Whether you're reading this because you are doing great and want to continue doing well, you are doing okay and want to do better, or because you are struggling and want something more, Scripture holds up at every level, and research reinforces this truth.

My Not-So-Hidden Agenda

That's why I'm going to do everything I can to convince you to think about what you are thinking. I am going to encourage you to think about your marriage in much the same way happy couples think about theirs.

So, over the course of this book we will focus on becoming more intentional with the thoughts that impact your marriage, specifically your thoughts about yourself, your spouse, your spouse's emotions, your response, and the purpose of marriage. We will do this through the lens of research and the lens of what God thinks because we'll discover the two align more than we might have ever imagined.

Essentially, we are going to work to memorize **Five Intentional Thoughts** that have the potential to revitalize your marriage by revitalizing your thoughts. And these five thoughts are based on five verses, with the goal of setting your mind on having your best Us. This is crucial because ultimately you are the boss of your thoughts. You can boss them, versus them bossing you. No one ever told me that. That's why I'm telling you. Because that truth changed my life, changed my marriage, and has convinced me the same thing is possible for everyone.

But Where Do I Start?

In order for a change of mind to be possible, it's crucial you start in a very specific place. Changing your thoughts will require you to have a growth mindset versus a fixed mindset.

> **A growth mindset** says, "I'm open to the idea that my thinking may need adjustment."
>
> **A fixed mindset** says, "It is what it is."

The concept of a **growth and fixed mindset** was developed by psychologist Carol Dweck and popularized in her book, *Mindset: The New Psychology of Success*.[3] Dr. Dweck's work on understanding the difference between growth and fixed mindsets was a huge "Aha!" for me. It helped explain the three mysteries I mentioned at the start—the puzzles I just couldn't get to the bottom of. It explained why some people change from marriage enrichment and others don't. It helped me see why some take advice while others don't and why some people are happy and others are not. This one difference was crucial to whether a lasting change was not only possible, but probable. A growth mindset is a must for a great marriage. Even if you are struggling, *especially if you are struggling*, would you be open to having a growth mindset? If you are still not convinced why this matters, let me give you a few real-life stories of the power of a mindset shift.

"We Know Tragedy and This Ain't It."

Over the course of our marriage, two of my close family members died within a two-year period. One was twenty-six and one was forty-nine. I was devastated, to say the least. It was tragic in every sense of the word.

As a result of experiencing such loss and pain in that season, somewhere along the way, Nancie and I started using the phrase, "We know tragedy and this ain't it." We said this because we *had* known tragedy. We had known explainable and—what felt like—unending grief. So, when faced with situations or difficulties that were challenging and asked a lot of us, as tempting as it was to catastrophize the moment, instead, we started to repeat: "We know tragedy and this ain't it."

Yes, things can be challenging. But most things aren't tragic. They are difficult. They ask a lot of us. They are inconvenient. But they aren't the end of the world. This little phrase gave us perspective that sometimes being in the middle of a tough time can cause us to miss. It's brought insight to our family and helped us prioritize what is worthy of concern and what isn't.

Nancie has adopted the use of this phrase with surgical precision. A few years back, my daughter joined me on a speaking trip. I booked a hotel, but when we got there, I discovered I had booked it for the wrong night. At first this didn't seem to be a problem, because they still had a room available for the night we needed it. Then came the catch. The rate was double. It was a nicer than normal hotel for us. In fact, it was so expensive that under normal circumstances I would have never paid that rate. (Nancie would FOR SURE never have paid that rate.) But, due to the hotel's no-refund policy, I had no choice but to take the room.

Here's the relational math: My mistake, plus Nancie's shrewdness with money, could have equaled her saying, "Are you kidding me right now?" Instead, when I called, her response to my mistake was, "Hey, we know tragedy and this *ain't* it."

Nancie would have been justified if she had gotten frustrated with me. She could have made me feel bad about it. But truly, she didn't need to. I *already* felt bad about it. Plus, responding in a way to make me feel bad is not a great marriage move, it's a poor parenting move. Instead, she leveraged the situation to communicate unconditional love and grace. My daughter and I were able to enjoy our trip because my wife didn't pile on about the mistake I made.

While a mistake booking a hotel room is a smallish example, that's exactly the point. Most of our married-people frustrations are made up of conflicts that are "smallish". Your spouse makes a mistake. You make mistakes. That's a given. But your mindset towards their mistakes is not a given. You get to choose that. And what you choose will determine your response. Thankfully because these mistakes happen all the time in marriage, you will have the chance over and over again to shift the way you see them, remembering, your mindset towards your spouse's mistakes really matters.

"Rich People Problems"

Here's another example of a mindset shift. Over the years, a helpful perspective building term has evolved: "rich people problems". If you make over $30,000 a year, you are richer than almost 80% of the people on the planet.[4] In light of that, not having good Internet service in parts of your house, not being able to take a "nice" vacation, not being able to upgrade your iPhone, should all be viewed as rich people problems. This is stuff most of the world will never have the opportunity to deal with!

This idea has really resonated in our marriage and become a part of a mindset shift in our home. We agreed to stop complaining about rich people problems. When we did this, our problems, in light of real problems in the world, started to seem really small. While we are not perfect at it, it has wiped out many frustrations at the Lowe house and has stopped many of our complaints in mid-sentence. In other words, our situations haven't changed, our *mindsets* have changed, and it has mattered more than we could have guessed.

"What If I Had Let Her Go?"

One more example of a perspective change. After speaking at a marriage event recently, a man named Brent approached me in the lobby to tell me his story. He started with, "Your marriage study saved our marriage." Prior to the study, Brent and his wife's marriage story included infertility challenges and losing a baby in the 8th month of pregnancy that also almost resulted in the loss of his wife, Veronica. The loss of their child devastated them both, but their reactions were different. She was devastated and angry. He was devastated and withdrawn. As a result of their differing grieving styles, the tension grew between them. He said he just didn't know how to love her through it. He reasoned it would be better to let her go so she could find someone who could "love her better." Veronica insisted they go to the marriage study at their church.

His mindset was, "How is that going to help?" Then he laughed and said to me, "Boy was I wrong."

Brent went on to tell me how his mind had shifted on a few key marital habits. He learned through the study that his wife just wanted his presence. She didn't really want him to do anything other than just be with her. That simple piece of wisdom, to just be there with her, changed everything; *and it all started by changing what he thought he should do with her pain*. It started with him changing his mind. His wife, Veronica, walked up during my conversation with her husband. I will never forget the moment when, in mid-sentence with me, he stopped what he was saying, gently pulled her to him, and said, "What if I had let her go? I just love her so much." She smiled at him and joined our conversation saying, "We're not perfect. But it's different. It's a different way of handling our anger, our hurts. Life can be better, so much better." I still get chills as I type this. This couple, struggling after a tremendous loss, briefly paused their lives and changed their minds about their marriage. And changing their minds literally saved their marriage.

I could keep going, but you get the idea. A shift in mindset can be the shift your marriage needs if you are in crisis, need help dealing with a specific issue, or to take your marriage from "just okay" to "great!". But for that shift to happen, you must be honest with yourself about your thinking. Here's where we move from just good ideas to diving in to make your marriage the best it can be.

So, What About You?

Imagine you and I sitting down over coffee, and me asking you the following questions:

- What do you think about yourself?
- What do you think about your spouse?
- What do you think about your spouse's emotions?
- What do you think about your response?
- What do you think is the purpose of your marriage?

As you think about those questions, what feelings come up? What thoughts come up? What are you feeling in your body? Can you see how the answers to these questions are so critical? Can you see how your thoughts determine your actions and approach?

I realize these are huge questions with huge implications, and that's the point. But please let me encourage you that no matter where you are in your marriage, I am for you. And I need you to hear me: we are going to take this one step at a time. I promise, I'm not going to beat you up; my intention is to build you up. As much as I can, I'm going to try to make you laugh. And most importantly, I've included space in this book for you to... Think About It.

In each chapter you will find a Think About It section. This will give you a chance to start to become more intentional with your thoughts. I know every author says this, but please don't skip this part. This is where everything becomes personal to you and your marriage. This section will not take a lot of time, just some honesty and self-awareness. Plus, it may be one of the most important things you ever do for your marriage. Let's practice just a bit now. Take a few minutes and think through—maybe even write down—the answers to these questions:

Think About It

What are you hoping to get from this book?

What about this book and this process scares you?

....

What would be a win for your marriage on the other side of reading this book?

....

....

....

....

The Payoff

Despite any hesitations, can I humbly ask, what do you have to lose by believing a change is possible? By having a growth mindset about your marriage? Better question: what might you gain with a growth mindset? Just think, if you apply one truth from this book, it will be worth the time it takes to read it. So, I want you to take a deep breath, right now. We are going to have a good time, and your marriage is going to be better for it. Changing your mind with a few thoughts is easier than you think. Promise.

ADHD SIDE SQUIRREL ALERT: Wait, hold on, stapler lady just stood up. She must be out of staples. She's gathering her things, she's packing up... she just slammed her chair into the table. She seems angry at her shortage of office supplies. I didn't think anger was allowed in a place where the slogan is "Shhhh." But praise the Lord, she is leaving! I wish her well and hope to never see her again. She and her stapler are gone! God's fist-bump for the day.

Sorry for the distraction, let's do this.

Chapter Two

What Do You Think About Yourself?

I LIKE PEOPLE. I DO. I'm fascinated with how differently people are wired. I believe everyone has a fascinating story, and I love to hear them tell it. Nancie said to me once, "I love this about you, and I wouldn't change it, but I think you like people most people don't." I said, "Put that on my tombstone: Here lies Ted Lowe. He even liked you."

But even I have my limits. There is one person who has always been in my life, who can push my buttons now, but used to drive me crazy all day every day. Let me just keep it real. He can talk way too much. He once told me, "I talk to think," to which I thought, "No kidding." The way he phrases things sometimes just annoys me. I can dwell on it for days, even years. And he can rehash the same thing over and over. I think the reason he rehashes everything is because of another thing he does that drives me crazy: he can be paralyzed by decisions. It can take him forever to make decisions, even simple ones. He also—and this may sound petty, but it's super annoying—misplaces things *all the time*. He's always asking, "Hey, can you call my phone?" This makes no sense to me. Our phones have become part of our bodies, it's like saying, "Hey can you call my hand?" For these shallow reasons and deeper reasons, until recently, I had a really hard time liking him. So, who is this guy?

This guy is me.

I used to really struggle with how I think about myself. This has been the case my entire life, even as a kid, especially as a teenager and young adult, and yes, even now.

In fact, I've named the speaker of these negative thoughts in my mind, Fred. Fred in my head. And let me say in the kindest way possible, Fred is a jerk. He says things to me I would never say to anyone else...ever!

Fred Franchises

I have found many people have their own Fred in their heads. Do you? If so, does he criticize your appearance, your parenting, your intelligence, your social skills, your work, your home, your lawn, your finances, your athletic ability (or lack thereof)? Does he leverage social media to show you how you don't measure up? Does he take someone else's good news and make you feel bad? Does he do that sadistically magical thing of making you feel anxious, depressed, and helpless, while simultaneously making you feel 100% responsible to fix it? Does he encourage you to dwell on the regrets of the past or fears of the future? Does he create a coating that repels compliments like a Scotchgard™ coating on a new couch? Is he the anxious engine that drives you at work, home, and even play? Is he wearing you down and wearing you out? Does he encourage you to numb out in unhealthy ways, then afterwards tell you that was unforgivable? Is he making you irritable, selfish, self-protective, no fun?

Or maybe your Fred is a different kind of jerk. Maybe he tells you, you are the hero of every story, even stories where you aren't. Maybe he makes you think more highly of yourself than you should. Does he tell you your problems are other people's fault? Does he tell you your life is unfair? Has he mastered the blame game? Maybe his tone is frustrated, arrogant, and angry at others, constantly saying, "Nobody understands you. You know so much more. Why don't they just listen to you? You are so right. They are so wrong. If only they would do it your way, this would all be better." Perhaps, your Fred's goal is to make you just like him: frustrated, angry, on edge, out of patience, and out of love.

So, What Does This Have to Do with Marriage?

Fred's words can make you nervous, anxious, insecure, worried, frustrated, and lonely—which aren't exactly adjectives that describe a spouse ready to love and serve, or even able to *receive* love for that matter.

Let me give you a couple of examples of how Fred works:

- Imagine you are scrolling on your phone and you see a social media post of a friend from high school. Fred compares your life to theirs and declares you the loser. After hearing that, now imagine your spouse walking in to discuss the credit card bill. How do you think that is going to go? Fred has officially set up that conversation to lose.

- Imagine driving home from work while Fred tells you you're lousy at your job, nobody understands you, and that you are probably going to be out of a job soon. After hearing those words, now imagine walking through the door and seeing your spouse. With these thoughts still rolling in your head, do you think you will be excited to see your spouse? Ready to listen about their day? Ready to serve them? Probably not. Fred, at the very least, has ruined your evening with your spouse.

When we listen to Fred, it's painful. This pain can make us selfish, which means our spouse is living with someone who is, at least at times, selfish. So, we often end up trying to get from our spouse what our spouse was never intended to give us. They were not meant to—nor are they able to—meet all our emotional needs. To expect them to is not only unfair, it's impossible. For many, Fred leads us to think our spouse has what we need, but they just won't give it to us—even if we don't know what it is.

For some of us, the fears Fred whispers can make us defensive. For others of us, his whispers lead us to escape physically or emotionally. For others, his whispers lead us to be more controlling of our spouse. For some, his whispers keep us from doing little more than existing. In all of those scenarios, our spouse misses out on living with someone who is loved—secure in a love that never, no matter what, changes.

But, **the most concerning thing about Fred is that he can become louder than the voice of God**. And when that happens, those around us miss out on who we are when we feel safe and loved—the best version of ourselves.

A Look Inside

I realize some people have a larger struggle with Fred than others. But I think the conversation of how you think about yourself is essential for all of us. For me, it's been a significant struggle.

I struggled with whether to share this next part with you or not—Fred passionately tried to talk me out of it. But my wife passionately tried to talk me into it. Nancie wins. In the first chapter, I teased about having ADHD. But on top of my ADHD, I've also struggled with anxiety. While I would say I'm productive, loving, and relational, the struggle is real and at times has been relentless. The pain got so real in 2001, I had to do something about it. I finally reached out to a counselor. It helped a lot. In fact, I've seen a counselor off and on ever since. I've also taken medications and supplements since I started getting help. In addition, I've leveraged my favorite natural medication since college: exercise. All these things have helped me dramatically, but I decided to take it a step further. I wanted to see Fred for myself. So, I gave myself a gift: brain scans. I will explain, but before I do, I want you to know, yes, I did the scans for me. But I also did them for this book. So, at the risk of sounding smarmy, I did them for you too.

The purpose of brain scans is to determine the health and challenges of the brain. For the majority of psychiatrists, their treatment recommendations are based on the symptoms reported to them by their patients. Psychiatrist, Dr. Daniel Amen, and the psychiatrists in his clinic do something different. They base their treatment recommendations on the reported symptoms AND brain scans.

The Results

Much of the brain scan interpretations are focused on the levels of blood flow. Problems often stem from having too much or too little blood flow in certain areas of the brain. For instance, there is an area of the brain called the deep limbic system. The deep limbic system is responsible for translating our emotional state into physical feelings of relaxation or tension. The scans revealed I have too much blood flow in my deep limbic system. The doctor explained that for many, too much blood flow in the deep limbic system can cause depression, anxiety, and ruminating, negative thoughts. When he said the words, "ruminating, negative thoughts," I checked out for a moment and had ruminating, negative thoughts about having ruminating, negative thoughts.

Those three words seemed to define Fred's mission. For many years, I would get stuck on negative thoughts and allow them to berate me. For example, when I was fourteen, I had a distant relative ask me how old I was. I was with a group of other kids when he asked. I guess to get a laugh I said, "I'm fourteen. How old are you?" The man shot me a look that communicated what I knew the moment after I said it: that was *not* funny. That was disrespectful. The memory of saying that can still cause a visceral response in me to this day. Now, that is not the worst thing I've ever said, trust me! But it's an example of how my mind can work, and maybe yours too. If your Fred is like mine, he keeps meticulous, permanent recordings that he plays at all the wrong times.

Nervous Nelson

There's another area of my brain with too much blood flow that Fred leverages: the basal ganglia. Too much blood flow there causes nervous energy. Nervous energy is on-brand for me. Fidgeting is my jam. I tinker with my phone case constantly. Sitting still usually isn't an option for me. But make no mistake about it, I use this nervous energy to get things done. I've made it work for me at work. It's helped me, ironically, to write this book. I've made it work for me at home too. I can knock out a Saturday home project like an HGTV crew hyped up on Red Bull. But I can wear myself out. I'm a lot—or as my oldest daughter would say, I'm *"extra."* Seeing these brain scans explained why I used to say to my wife about my mind, "It's hard to be in here."

Brain Change

But there is a massive amount of hope. Despite the problematic blood rush into the wrong areas of my brain, I have to say, God has put great people, principles, and habits in my life that have helped deal with the lies ruminating in my head (aka, Fred). And now I want to share them with you. I want you to experience what it is like to live with Fred in his proper place. So, let's do this. Let's begin getting your Fred out of your head.

Right now, I want you to imagine your Fred has just said something nasty to you.

Now take Fred by the earlobe and drag him to the side and say, "I'm turning you off and I'm hearing from someone else." Now take a deep breath and let this wash over you:

> *The Spirit you received does not make you slaves, so that you live in fear again; rather, the Spirit you received brought about your adoption to sonship. And by him we cry, "Abba, Father." (Romans 8:15 NIV)*

Now imagine a loving parent taking your face in their hands, looking you in the eye and saying, "Those negative thoughts you wrote down, those aren't from Me. You are not __________, __________, __________. You are mine. You don't have to be afraid. I've called you by name, you are my child. Don't miss Me. Don't do life alone. I'm right here for you."

You Are Worth A Lot

God says you have infinite value. Nothing you've said or done can add or subtract to what has already been determined to be true of you. You are loved. You are valued. You are accepted. You matter.

I know that changing your thoughts can feel challenging. But I hope these verses at least encourage you in knowing that what feels challenging to you now, has been a challenge since the beginning of humanity. That verse we just read from a letter the apostle Paul wrote to the church in Rome tells us that even ancient people understood this problem. You aren't alone. The people Paul is writing to in Rome get it. Their neural pathways had been carved out to believe life was about doing all the right things and not doing all the wrong things. To be asked to shift their minds from that continual angst to the radical love of God, was a huge leap for their minds to make. Living like a child who is unconditionally loved is hard to wrap our minds around too. It is hard to believe, much less live out. But, it's not impossible.

I want to look again at Romans 8:15. Paul writes, *"The Spirit you received does not make you slaves, so that you live in fear again..."* The word "spirit," the second word in Romans 8:15, is translated as "dominant frame of mind."[3] Think about that for a second. God does not want our **dominant frame of mind** to be fear, but that of a safe, well-loved, well-cared for son or daughter.

But here's the thing. You will be surrounded by voices (including your own) who will work to tell you otherwise. They will be persuasive. They will be loud. They will be insistent. But when we follow Jesus, when we believe we are who God says we are, we can put the voices that say otherwise where they belong.

Who Is Rolling Round in Your Head?

So, the question is: Who is running the dominant frame of your mind? Is it your Fred or God? Is your dominant frame of mind fear or love? Fear tells us we are alone, not enough, never going to measure up, and must fight to be accepted. That fear keeps us on a hamster wheel of effort and exhaustion that never takes us where we were meant to be. Our fear derives from all sorts of things. When you think about what fears drive you, what fear does Fred use on you most often? Is it:

- being wrong,
- appearing lazy,
- being unloved,
- feeling unwanted,

- feeling worthless,
- being disrespected,
- lacking purpose,
- not knowing,
- experiencing chaos,
- being deprived?

Regardless of our primary fears, the result is the same. We forget we belong to God. And we forget we are radically loved by God.

Now What?

Knowing Fred can't be trusted is important, but we have to know how to combat what he says with what is true. When we focus, when we remember who we are, it matters. When you say, out loud or to yourself: "Remember who I am," there's an impact. It soothes. It matters to our souls, our brains, and our bodies. Romans 8:6 reminds us:

> *The mind governed by the flesh is death, but the mind governed by the Spirit is life and peace.*

There is life and peace when we listen to God instead of the voice of Fred.

When we remember who we are and Whose we are, we remember...

- A child of God can lean into the Father's grace and mercy, knowing God has a plan.
- A child of God knows she is not alone.
- A child of God can breathe.
- A child of God can be still and know that God is God.
- A child of God doesn't try to get his spouse to meet all his needs.
- A child of God can find *peace*.

Paul is saying, the Spirit of God that lives in you isn't passive, or even a nicer version of you. As followers of Jesus, we have the Holy Spirit to counsel us with grace and truth. When we recognize the Holy Spirit's voice, we recognize the voice of God in us and through us. Peace is possible. I didn't think I could ever have this peace. Maybe you feel the same. If you do, don't give up. If I can find it, you can too.

Ask Yourself...

When you think about how you think about yourself, what lens are you thinking through?

Through the lens of love or through the lens of fear?

Do you feel like you have something to prove, something to earn, something to do to get the love you want?

Or do you see yourself as God sees you? Infinitely loved with a place to belong? Accepted. Safe. Your brain needs to know this because when your brain knows this, your body can sense it. And that means the people around you can sense it too.

What I Am Not Saying

While I believe beginning to internalize how deeply loved we are by God is a deeply spiritual practice, I am not saying if you are hearing Fred on the regular, it's because you aren't spiritual enough. In fact, I love that in recent years many Christian leaders, speakers, and authors have stopped telling people with depression, anxiety, and other challenges that they just need to "pray more". This message to just pray away mental illness has been a dangerous one, so I love that we are finally lovingly and intelligently addressing our mental health and thought lives in a more holistic way.

That being said, we have to be careful not to inadvertently belittle the power of what happens when we individually stop and talk with the One who loves us most. So, I want to caution you not to just accept your Fred as part of you—believing he represents a wiring in you that you won't ever be able to change, or that can't ever be dealt with. Because here is the thing; with acceptance comes surrender. The advantage of surrender is that you stop blaming yourself for everything. The caution with surrender is the powerlessness you can feel.

What I Didn't See Coming

When I first saw my brain scans, I had a moment where I felt like I could finally stop beating myself up for my ADHD and anxiety. *Those things are not my fault. And the same thing is true for millions of people who struggle with brain health.* In fact, I chose, in part, to do the brain scans because I wanted to finally confirm to myself that my struggles were not because of a character flaw. The brain scans did that and I was—and continue to be—so thankful. But for at least a month following my brain scans, I experienced something I had not anticipated. Fred used the findings from my brain scans to hurt me in a new way. "See?" he told me. "You are so broken. Your brain is defective. You will struggle forever. Maybe you aren't as functional as you think. Maybe, unlike you, everyone else can see how broken you really are." I had ruminating thoughts about having ruminating thoughts. Fred said, "This is too big for you." And here was the scariest thing he said: "This is too big for Jesus and any of the other things you do to keep me at bay." You can imagine how powerless this made me feel.

What I Am Saying

But the truth is, regardless of what your Fred is telling you and my Fred is telling me, no matter how hard it can be to be in our body, Jesus still matters. Jesus still gets the final word about who you are and what you're worth.

Yes, you may need to take medication and supplements. I do. Yes, you need to be intentional with your diet, exercise, breathing, and sleep. I am. But Jesus in your head matters. You can choose to remember who you are.

While I don't think many of us are going to know complete peace on this side of heaven, remembering Jesus is with us in the midst of it all is no small thing. That word we see pop up around Christmas time, Immanuel, is not just something that matters every December. Immanuel, meaning *God with us*, is a truth we can stake our lives on. And it changes everything. No matter how overwhelming Fred's voice, no matter how impossible it seems to silence his incessant badgering, the truth of *God with us*, reminds us we do not fight this mental battle alone.

Presence Matters

God with us matters like a parent's presence matters to a sick child. To a child who is sick, a parent being there matters, regardless if he or she ever gets well. A parent's presence amid their child's pain doesn't fix the illness, but it could not be more essential. It reassures them in a very tangible way that they aren't alone.

I've seen this truth play out in real ways every summer. Our family volunteers with an amazing organization called Lighthouse Family Retreat that provides summertime retreats for families who are living with childhood cancer. When you talk with the parents about their child's illness, they sound like medical professionals. The number of hours they have spent in hospitals and doctor's offices is obvious because of how well-informed they are about every detail of the disease and the treatments. And they have to be well-informed because by knowing everything, they can be the best possible advocates for their children.

But even more than knowing incredible amounts of information, through the entire childhood cancer journey, these parents are there with their children. The hours caring for sick kids is exhausting, but these parents fight through it to be there for and with their kids. Of course they do. These are their babies. These babies dazzled and exhausted their parents as newborns. They watched them take first steps, throw up in odd places and do things they would swear no child has ever done before. As the saying goes, children are your heart walking outside of your body. So, of course, there is just no question that they will be there with and for their children.

And that is exactly how God feels about you and me. We get to call God, Abba, Father. I'm not sure how to wrap my non-neurotypical brain around all that, but it's powerful nonetheless.

And that is why the first of the **Five Intentional Thoughts** I want to encourage you to incorporate into your thinking is this:

INTENTIONAL THOUGHT #1

⇨ "Remember who I am."

You can choose to remember to say to your Fred, and to yourself anytime you have a hard time believing the truth:

"Remember who I am."

When we remember who we are, when we compare what Fred says to us versus what God says about us, the contrast couldn't be greater. What Fred says diminishes us. What God says delivers us. That is why it is worth it to do what I'm about to ask you to do.

Earlier, I asked you to write down a negative thought about yourself. Now I'm going to ask you to take it a step further. I'm going to challenge you to do something that will help you get even more specific. It may bring up uncomfortable feelings. And if you are like me, feelings are not always welcomed, wanted, or convenient. There's a reason we dance around them, drown them out, or as I do, try to literally outrun them. But I want to ask you to be brave for a moment. The pay-off can be huge. It has been for me, and I want that for you. So I'm going to ask you to do an exercise that has changed my life. (And please don't do that thing I do with books and skip the interactive part.) This is the part that rewires your brain for the better, and lets Fred know his days of being in power are over. Please do not skip this part.

Think About It

⇨ Remember Who I Am

Step 1: Name Your Fred

I want to encourage you to bundle your negative thoughts about yourself and give him or her a name. You can call yours Fred if you like. I'm certain Fred is agreeable to franchising. Or you can give her or him a name that has meaning or humor to you. Giving him a name is one of the most powerful things you can do to battle Fred. It simultaneously makes him more and less important. Naming him helps acknowledge the importance of your thoughts, while also separating those thoughts from who you really are. At the same time, naming him also helps make him a joke, and for many of us, humor heals. Now it's your turn.

Write down the name of your Fred:

Step 2: Write Fred's Messages to You

Below is some space to write down some of the negative and worrisome thoughts that come from Fred.

If you are like me and prefer more privacy, write them on a separate piece of paper or in a document in your computer labeled, "ToDoforWork," nobody will want to read that. Give yourself at least 10 minutes to sit in this question. Don't hurry past it. If we are going to put Fred in his proper place, we need to know exactly what kind of thoughts we are listening for.

....

....

....

....

....

Step 3: Talk Back to Fred

Fred is very crafty and has many side-hustles. In addition to the thoughts above, check which of the following roles Fred has played in those thoughts.

- ○ Fortune Teller (I know the future)
- ○ Mind Reader (I know what they are thinking)
- ○ Interpreter (I know what all that really means)
- ○ Shamer (I can't believe you did that)
- ○ Labeler (You are ....)
- ○ Blamer (He/She is responsible!)
- ○ Convincer (You should just go ahead and ....)

- ○ Guilter (How can you live with yourself?)
- ○ Always/Never'er (This is never going to get better, because you always and/or never ....)
- ○ **Step 4: Write God's Message to You**

Now ask yourself, what would a loving, perfect God say to you? Then write it below. (Need help knowing what God would say? See the Appendix on page 127. There you will find verses to remind you who you are.)

....

....

....

....

Repeat the exercise above for one week. (My hunch is, it won't be the last week you do it.)

Why This Matters So Much

While most of us can agree that Fred isn't the voice we want speaking into our lives, it isn't enough to just decide to stop listening to him. We have to acknowledge, categorize, and challenge Fred with the truths of God. We have to replace one with the other. When we do that, we begin reflecting more of what God is like. We become more loving, joyful, peaceful, patient, kind, good, faithful, gentle, and self-controlled. Who doesn't want that for themselves—and who doesn't want that in a spouse and for their spouse?

That is why I started a marriage book with what you think about yourself as an individual. **What you think about *yourself* radically determines how your spouse experiences you—and that radically effects your marriage.** Now that you have a way of dealing with your Fred, imagine moments before reconnecting with your spouse at the end of the day, that Fred belittles you. Now imagine saying out loud—if possible—*Remember who I am. No, I am not perfect. But I am also not stupid. I am loved by God and now I will love my spouse.* These few thoughts can change your brain and your body and who your spouse will experience when you walk through the door. **What you think about you changes everything about you.** So, let's **test and approve** those thoughts, because it matters to everything we value, including our *Us*.

I've done a similar exercise popularized by Dr. Daniel Amen, and originally created by Aaron Beck, MD, founder of cognitive therapy, called ANTS (Automatic Negative Thoughts) Therapy. And believe me when I tell you, it works. Not only that, the data says it has worked for thousands of people. The last step of ANTS therapy is talking back to your negative thoughts. That is powerful, but for me, I like to go one step further and allow God to talk back to my negative thoughts. Inviting God and Scripture into this equation has been a game changer.

Often the results of the exercise can be pretty instant. But it is not easy. Fred has created these negative neural pathways and we have to create new ones. In fact, I have to remind myself daily, sometimes repeatedly throughout the day, *who I am*. That's okay. That's the way my brain is wired. And I never thought I would say this, but my brain being wired this way is actually a gift. It makes me dependent on the One who loves me most. It keeps me coming back to God and relying on God in a way I never have before. Me dealing with Fred has made more space and room for God to speak to me. Here are a few one-liners from Fred and the thoughts I now intentionally use instead:

Fred: "You will always have to work by yourself."

New Message: "I am not alone. I have many people who help me do what God has called me to do. (i.e. For one, my friend and coworker, Sarah—who is editing this book!)"

Fred: "Other people are accomplishing so much more than you."

New Message: "Do your best and trust God with the outcome."

Fred: "Don't ever forget that terrible thing he said to you."

New Message: "Practice forgiveness and don't give God-size power to people."

It's amazing how just a few intentional thoughts can change my outlook, how I function, who I am...who Nancie lives with!

Another thing that has helped with Fred is cluing other people into him. After speaking engagements is typically the time Fred is the most brutal with me. He tells me all of the things I shouldn't have said and all the things I should have said. He highlights all my mistakes. Now that I'm teaching others about Fred, people encourage me afterwards with things like, "Don't listen to Fred. That was great stuff."

Again, the counseling, diet, sleep, exercise, and sharing it with others matters greatly to my ability to drown out Fred. And I CANNOT encourage you enough to take care of yourself. But I must say, as clearly as I possibly can, Jesus in my head reminding me who I really am and who I really am not, is the thing that saves me and delights me daily. My brain scans show that from a neurological perspective, the peace, joy, love, and contentment I have found shouldn't be possible. But God's people, God's Word, and God's principles have become louder than the neurological make-up of my brain. Jesus rescued me from the ruminating thoughts I have about myself—good or bad—and my brain requires that I allow Jesus to rescue my mind, *daily*. In other words, the phrase: "If I can do it, anybody can do it," REALLY applies in this case. When I say I'm on this journey with you, *I'm really on this journey with you*, by choice, by necessity, every day.

Open Your Hands

But I forget sometimes. I forget to challenge Fred. You too may forget sometimes. In fact, we are not unlike the children my friend, Leslie, works with. She serves families who have adopted children from developing countries who, as you might imagine, have unique challenges. Leslie shared about one family she worked with in particular who adopted their son from Romania. For years, when they checked on him after he had fallen asleep, they would find food clenched in his fists. Even though he had plenty of food in his new home, even though he was safe, even though he was loved in every way, his past life told him he still had to look out for himself, even as he slept. It was hardwired into his brain, and I would dare say his heart. But as their son continued to experience his parents' love, his food insecurity began to go away. His fists were open during the day and night and so was his heart and his mind. He finally knew he didn't have to do it all on his own. He was always safe and loved. He finally started to live like he believed it was true.

The same is true for you. You have always been loved. No matter what your Fred says, you are. Changing life-long brain pathways does not happen overnight. But they can change. You can start living like this is true. We can have the same spirit described in 2 Timothy 2:7:

> *For God has not given us the spirit of fear, but of power, and love, and self-control (ESV).*

Power, love, and self-control? Doesn't that sound like something your life and your marriage could use some more of? I know it does to me.

Before You Turn the Page

If you raced through the **Think About It** section, I implore you to plan a time to go back and do it. Just give it five minutes. Nothing has helped me battle Fred like this exercise, and I'm not the only one.

Since teaching this material live, I've been blown away with the conversations I've had with people afterward. A guy—I'll call him Joe—approached me after I had presented the session about how we battle Fred by remembering who you are. He asked if we could meet in private.

When we met, Joe, a basketball coach of a major university, told me about his Fred. Despite Joe's stellar record of wins for many years, Joe said his Fred always told him it wasn't good enough. But he didn't just stop there. Fred said the same type of things to him about all areas of his life. Fred berated Joe as a husband, father, and friend. In fact, Joe had gotten up early that morning and ran a seven-minute mile and he told me that Fred had said when he finished, "If you had hustled around that curve you would have finally beaten this seven minute mile you are stuck at."

I could relate to everything Joe was telling me. Fred said and can still say the same sorts of things about me...in every area of my life. Since the event where Joe and I first met, we've kept in touch. Recently I asked him if this exercise is helping with his Fred, and he said, "I can't believe how much it is!" Joe discovered that dealing with Fred is not only good for him, it's good for his wife. When I talked with Joe's wife, I told her we were going to get Fred out of Joe's head. She responded with, "What a gift that would be. He is so hard on himself. I would love that for him." See, she has seen the toll Fred has taken on her husband. She has seen Fred literally steal Joe's victories on every level. And when Fred starts to fade in Joe's mind, she too will reap the rewards of living with a man who remembers who he is.

My prayer for Joe is the same prayer I have for you, too: Remember Whose and who you are.

(And if you still haven't done the exercise earlier in the chapter, now's your chance.)

Chapter Three

What Do You Think About Your Spouse?

PEOPLE SAY MARRIAGE IS SO COMPLICATED. And while I think we are all complicated people, I don't think how we love is always as complicated as we make it out to be. It's just not always easy. I think the more accurate description is this: **marriage is so close.** Two people become one person—it doesn't get any closer than that.

When we get married, we put ourselves in close proximity to our spouse in every way. Everything about you and everything about them collides. Your differences and similarities are now in ultra-close proximity. Even our stuff has to find a way to get along. I was more prepared for this part of our marriage because I watched my step-mom, Diane, masterfully blend her family's stuff and my dad's family's stuff when they got married.

My mom passed away when I was 10. This left my 12-year-old-brother, my Dad, and me, home alone for eight years. We were like bears with a house. My dad and Diane married the summer after I graduated high school. We lived on a farm which meant my stepmom and stepbrothers had to move into the farmhouse with us. But when you read farmhouse, don't think Chip and Joanna Gaines. I don't know what I want you to think, but don't think Chip and Jo. My dad, brother, and I had not exactly been adding shiplap and carefully accessorized open shelving. But my sweet stepmom was about to change all that.

Whenever I came home from college, I was amazed at how she was transforming the bear cave into a lovely home. The house looked better every day but she did it in a kind, gentle, slowish way. But if there was one looming obstacle to Diane's much needed takeover it was the fact that my dad was a duck hunter and there were mounted ducks *all over* the family room walls. I couldn't wait to see how she would handle this. Turns out, she handled it like a blended family stuff ninja. On a visit home, I noticed that the ducks were flying on one wall. The next visit home I noticed they were flying closer and closer together. Then I noticed they were flying higher and to the left. Then they started to disappear one by one. Turns out they were flying south for the winter, and by south, I mean the basement. This was a few decades ago and I'm pretty sure my dad still hasn't noticed. So yes, when you get married, your stuff—from ducks to dishes—now belongs to your Us.

Even More Stuff

And it's not just our stuff. It's our *stuff*. We all bring baggage into marriage, figuratively and literally. Handling the figurative stuff can be even more confusing than handling stuffed waterfowl. You push buttons, they push buttons, and you are left wondering, what was all *that* about? Your differences are also having to dance on the regular. Perhaps you are extremely time-conscious while time is more of a loose construct for your spouse. Or maybe your extroverted spouse drags you to parties and your idea of a party is a party of one, two tops, four on New Year's Eve. Or maybe they like to talk about their feelings, all of them. While you would rather talk about your one feeling, never.

Or maybe the collision of the two of you has been a blast. You love their stuff and their *stuff*. Maybe you love having a dart board in your bedroom. Maybe you've learned to loosen up time restraints and live more in the moment. Maybe you realize you aren't as introverted as you thought. Or maybe they've helped you to see that you have more than one feeling. Who knew?

Regardless of whether the closeness of marriage has brought you closer together or pushed you farther apart, close proximity, plus personality, plus baggage, equals the narrative you are telling yourself about your spouse. **Everything they do impacts you.** These interactions come quick and often, and they start to inform what you think about your spouse and who you say they are as a person.

So, the question is: what are you telling yourself about your spouse? If you were writing a story, how would you describe them as a character? If they were in a Netflix series, what role would they play? It's crucial to know how we characterize our spouse because we operate as if it's the truth. And that's important because **how you think about your spouse will determine how you treat your spouse.**

For some of us, this is great news and explains why we treat our spouse so well. As I mentioned in chapter one, Dr. Helen Fisher's[2] study of couples who reported being madly in love after an average of 21 years, found one of the commonalities of happy couples' brains was an area of the brain responsible for *positive illusion*. Positive illusion is the ability to focus on what you love about your spouse, and *not* focus on what you don't. And this positive illusion does so much for everybody involved.

Positive illusion has been associated with:

- Higher marital satisfaction
- Higher personal satisfaction
- Decreased risk of relationship ending
- Less conflict
- Less doubt
- Higher sense of security
- Regulated feelings regarding the relationship
- Lasting intimacy [2]

Happy couples get this. They look at their spouse and see awesomeness. But you may be thinking, "I don't have those thoughts about my spouse because my spouse isn't awesome. They have huge flaws." You may be right and I will get back to you on that. **Still, while everyone is married to a flawed person, quite often the problem we have with the way we see our spouse has more to do with proximity to them than their actual flaws.**

Here's the real problem. Ready? The real problem is that often your spouse can get in *the way* of you getting *your way*. I know, that's tough to hear. But isn't it true? No one has the opportunity to get in your way more than your spouse. James, the brother of Jesus, actually talked about this very thing. In James 4:1–2 (MSG) he writes:

> *Where do you think all these appalling wars and quarrels come from? Do you think they just happen? Think again. They come about because you want your own way, and fight for it deep inside yourselves.*

Why do we get so frustrated with our spouse? Why do we think of them negatively? Often, it's because we want our own way and they keep us from getting it. We fight for our way deep inside ourselves, in our minds, in our thoughts and anyone who stands in our way can easily become our enemy. This becomes a dangerous mental game, a game most of us aren't aware we're playing. The game is called confirmation bias.

Confirmation bias is the tendency to interpret new evidence as confirmation of the beliefs one already holds. More simply put, **you find what you are looking for.** With confirmation bias, we make a decision and then look for evidence to validate our decision. This happens in marriage when we assign negative feelings to our spouse's words and actions.

For example, Blake says, "She's so lazy!" If he has *decided* his wife is lazy, he will look for the *evidence* to back that up and only see her napping on the couch, and NOT see her working 10 hours a day. Or Katie says "He's such a complainer!" If she has *decided* her husband is always complaining, she will hear words coming from his mouth that are negative. She won't notice the neutral or tender words that might be spoken throughout the day. Negative thoughts can cause you to act in a way that pushes your spouse away. This was the case for me during one of the toughest seasons in our marriage.

A Game with No Winners

Without realizing it, I was playing the game of confirmation bias. After four years of marriage, we moved from California to Georgia. When we first got to Georgia, I had underestimated how much I was going to miss our friends, my job, and the world's most perfect weather. At the time, I didn't realize I was struggling because of the loss of our lives in California. I thought I was struggling because I didn't like Georgia. One day, while mowing the lawn in 300-degree heat, my thoughts went a little something like this: "This is a big stupid lawn. Everyone said we would get a big huge lawn if we moved to Georgia. But this is dumb because now I have to mow this big stupid lawn. If I want some green space I can just go to a park. I don't need to own a park. It used to take me 10 minutes to mow our lawn in California, then we were off to the beach with friends. I don't really have friends here. I'm not sure I ever will. It's so hot, it's like Satan's breath out here. I hate it here. Nancie loves it here. She loves everything about this place. She's inside enjoying the cool. We talk like we both made the decision to move here, but I think she actually just convinced me to get what she wanted. In fact, I think she always gets what she wants. In fact, I think she is manipulative."

Labelmakers

What started out as frustration mowing my lawn turned into labeling Nancie as manipulative. I am not proud of those thoughts. But they seemed perfectly reasonable at the time. But today, they are painful to write. Maybe you relate. Perhaps you've had thoughts about your spouse that included labeling them.

The truth is, labels are a big deal. They make confirmation bias intentional and laser-focused. Think about it: how do you think I acted towards my wife when I came inside after mowing the grass? Do you think I was tender? Do you think I noticed if she was excited about something? Do you think I noticed if she was sad about something? Do you think I appreciated all she did for me? Do you think I noticed if she, God forbid, needed me? No, I didn't. Why? Because my thoughts had determined that the main character in my life was manipulative. Why would I do that to my own wife?! Why would I do that to myself? Why would I do that to

Us? Why? **Because I thought she had manipulated me out of getting my way.** As my friend Montell says, “If you can’t say amen, say ouch.”

So Much Hope

But here is the great news: If you have characterized your spouse in a negative light, the opposite of this principle is true. Positive thoughts equal positive actions equal connection. We can start—or continue—to think more positively towards our spouse with just a little intentionality. I have found the most effective way to focus your thoughts about your spouse is through the lens of Philippians 4:8. And this works if you follow Jesus or not. I call it the 4:8 filter.

> *Finally, brothers and sisters, whatever is true, whatever is noble, whatever is right, whatever is pure, whatever is lovely, whatever is admirable—if anything is excellent or praiseworthy—think about such things (Philippians 4:8 NIV).*

For all of you truth-tellers, and realists, I want to point out the first word on the list to guide your thoughts: true. God, in no way, wants you to live a lie. If you have been or are being hurt, that needs to be dealt with. Truth is a great protector for people. If a spouse is being abusive, then the truth confirms that is *never* okay. If a spouse has an addiction they refuse to deal with, then the truth is, something needs to change. So, take heart, this is not about seeing what is not there or ignoring something harmful. But the truth also helps acknowledge what is good about our spouse and our situation. We are never all one thing or the other. We are a complicated mix of good and bad, right and wrong, and to focus on the truth means we are able to acknowledge that both of those things exist in us and in our spouse. It also helps us ask ourselves: **Is this true about my spouse, or is the problem really about me not getting my way?** This is something we need to know and the 4:8 filter helps you know it.

Let’s Try Again

What if while I was mowing that day, I had used the 4:8 filter instead of just letting my mind run on auto-pilot? It would have looked something like this.

The 4:8 filter asks, *what is true?* And what is true is that we *both* decided to move to Georgia. Nancie may have wanted it more, but in no way did she coerce me. We had endless conversations about the pros and cons before making the decision to move. What else was true was that the location was not the problem. Grief was the problem; I was grieving my previous life. This was about so much more than mowing a large lawn. It was about acknowledging the sadness I felt over what was lost.

So, *true* is the first filter. The question of, *what is noble*, comes next. Nancie has proven over and over she is noble. She was noble when she left everything and everyone to follow me for the first five years of our marriage. She moved into my world in California. She was 23 years-old. That was a noble move that I benefited from greatly. The next question from the 4:8 filter is: *What is right?* The right thing was for me to tell her I was struggling without making her feel guilty or responsible. She didn't deserve my blame. That wasn't right for me to put it on her. Next, *what is pure?* The pure thing was for me to be gentle and compassionate and loving with her. *What is lovely?* What was lovely was Nancie's face. What was lovely was our new home and even our big stupid lawn. *What is admirable?* What was admirable was doing the right thing and loving her no matter my challenges.

My Pug

Had Philippians 4:8 been my filter that day I was mowing and melting in Georgia, how do you think I would have treated her differently than just allowing my thoughts to be on auto-pilot? What if my label had been what I've called her since 1995, Pug? Pug is my pet-name that somehow evolved from the pet-name of Pudding. Not only is Pug her pet-name. Pug is the main character in my life. Pug has my heart. In fact, I will often say, "You are my Pug." When she asks me why I love her the way I do, I will say, "Because you my Pug." (I ripped it off from Forrest Gump when Jenny asks him, "Forrest, why are you so good to me?" And he says, "Cause you my girl"). Now, when my kids see a man loving a woman in a movie, they will say, "That's his Pug!"

I have not been a perfect dad or husband, but my kids, family, and friends know I adore Nancie Hoblitzell Lowe, my Pug. She knows it too. Because I do. When I remember she is my Pug, I am more tender, more appreciative, and more available. When I characterize her as my Pug, when I think of her as my Pug, life is better. Because when I think better of Nancie, I love her better.

What Character Do You Have Your Spouse Playing?

How do you characterize your spouse? How can you recharacterize your spouse? Maybe that sounds like a strange question, but here is what I mean by that. What is the lens through which you see your spouse? What role do you have them playing in your marriage and in your life? And what might that role be keeping you and your marriage from becoming? Consequently, what area of your marriage do you need to run through the lens of Philippians 4:8? Maybe it's finances, sex, or your in-laws. Maybe it's chores, affection, future plans, or control. The point is to ask yourself, how can you reframe your thoughts in a true, but more positive light?

A New View

I saw a great example of someone recharacterizing their spouse with our friends, Payden and Lane. In addition to raising two young boys, Payden and Lane own and personally run a gym. Payden said she used to get so frustrated with how often Lane came home late. She said I was always thinking, "All day, I've handled the business side of the gym from home, all while taking care of the kids. I've made dinner. The kids want to see their dad and yet, he can't be bothered to be on time." In her mind, if the class was over at 7:00pm and it's a 15-minute commute, then he should be home by 7:30 at the latest. When he wasn't home by the time she thought he should be, she was cold to him when he finally did arrive. She would also make passive-aggressive comments about him always being late. When Lane would get there, dinner was on a plate, lights were off, kids were in bed, and Payden was watching TV or scrolling on her phone.

Inside she was hurt and mad because the narrative she had been telling herself was that he didn't care enough to come home on time. Then one night, after they had gone out and been able to connect on a date, she explained to him that it hurt her that he didn't make more of an effort to get home to her and the kids. She explained that it felt like he would rather be at the gym than with his family. He responded by saying that nothing could be further from the truth. He *wanted* to be home but felt a huge pressure to make the gym work to support their family.

Lane felt the thing that separated their gym from big chain gyms was personal attention and community. It was after training that people wanted to talk and that was typically late afternoons and early evenings. He said he felt torn between wanting to be home with the family and providing for the family. The honesty and vulnerability both Lane and Payden displayed in being willing to share their hurt and their fear was a game changer.

Payden was wise to dig beneath the anger to find the hurt that led to the truth. Lane was wise to reassure Payden instead of getting defensive.

Payden said this information not only led to more empathy (which we will dive into in the next chapter) but it also led to her characterizing her husband in a new way. Her thoughts around him totally changed. They still have the issue of her wanting him to spend more time with her and the boys, but now Payden approaches the tension thinking about what is true, noble, right, pure, lovely, admirable, excellent, and praiseworthy about Lane. And you know what? The list turns out to be pretty long. Her desire for him to be home did not change. Her need was still valid. But her approach and view of Lane was now poised to help the conversation create connection instead of disconnection.

Over the years, Payden and Lane have worked on the problem more constructively. They have struck a balance that works for the family. The business is more established now, employing more people who are able to stay late and talk with clients, so Lane can come home at a more consistent time. Sometimes when a later night is unavoidable Payden and the boys bring him dinner. The boys enjoy playing at the gym and Payden and Lane both get to connect with their clients in a more casual way. And when it is really important for him to be home at an exact time, she tells him in a different way.

Payden said, "Now when people tell me about a meaningful conversation Lane had with their teenager or about how they changed their mind about something after talking to Lane, I can hear their positive thoughts and feelings. Prior to that I would have rolled my eyes and thought, "Sure, he makes time to talk to you, but he's never home when I expect him to be." This solution, this connection, started with her seeking to think of her spouse in a more positive light. You and I can do the same. Changing how you think about your spouse can change how you treat your spouse. That is why I want you to incorporate the next intentional thought.

INTENTIONAL THOUGHT #2

⇨ "See the best."

When you are frustrated with your spouse, repeat to yourself—out loud if you can—*see the best* and then consider what that means.

A jumpstart on this practice would be to make a list of things you love about your spouse in general—out loud if you can. *See the best,* and then consider what that means. Training your mind to see the good in your spouse will begin to make that habit your default reaction. And to help do that, I want to encourage you to complete the exercise which will walk you through how to look at your spouse through the lens of Philippians 4:8.

Think About It

⇨ See the best

Fill in the following blanks and keep this list easily accessible, i.e. maybe take a photo and keep it on your phone. Fill in the list now, while also continuing to add to it in the coming days and weeks.

What is true about my spouse?

....

....

....

What is noble about my spouse?

What is right about our relationship?

What is pure about my spouse?

What is admirable about my spouse?

....

....

....

What is excellent about my spouse?

....

....

....

....

What is praiseworthy about my spouse?

....

....

....

....

Seeing Is Believing

Learning to see the best in our spouse is so powerful because it helps you to focus on what you love about your spouse and not focus on what you don't. Therapist Mark Kane Goldstein, conducted a study where he had couples keep a list of things that pleased them about their spouse. *Seventy percent* of couples who kept this kind of marriage diary reported an improvement in their relationship![5] What's magic about this was that nothing else changed other than their perception and focus. By doing this one simple thing they found their marriage was better than they had originally thought. They just had to start *looking* for what was good. Because when they looked for it, they found it, using their confirmation bias powers for good and not evil. They flexed the part of their brain that is responsible for positive illusion and everyone was better off as a result.

Again, this isn't about living in denial of the actual flaws you and your spouse have. It's about a change in perspective. The Philippians 4:8 filter gives us perspective on the big *and* the small things. The 4:8 filter reveals to us that we are flawed people married to flawed people, and we both have a lot of work to do on those flaws. And while annoying, the truth also tells us that those flaws are small. The small stuff is small stuff. As Nancie says, "Seeing the best helps eliminate the petty stuff."

When you are remembering what is true, noble, and right about your spouse, petty things matter less. When your spouse keeps arriving 10 minutes late, forgetting something at the supermarket, telling the same story twice, getting frustrated, falling asleep in the movie, breaking a dish, rolling their eyes, burping, talking too loud, and talking too little, those things simply don't matter as much. When you see the big picture of what you love about your spouse, it keeps the little annoying things from robbing the relationship. You let go of the dumb stuff that steals the joy from both of you, things that in the end, just...don't...matter! **Don't let the things that don't matter, matter to your marriage.**

Wait a Minute

You may be thinking, "But what if my spouse takes advantage of me choosing to look past the small stuff?" They could. But isn't it true that when people think you are great, and treat you like you are amazing, you are inclined to be kind to them, and not take advantage of them? We are drawn to the people who see the best in us! And even more than that, when I choose to see the best in my spouse, it makes my life infinitely better as well. In fact, in an interview, researcher Brene Brown said, "What if people are doing the best they can? I'll never know, but when I do, it makes my life better. To assume the best about people is almost an inherently selfish act because the life you change first is your own."[6] *Yes.*

Once again, Brené nails it.

The best part of the 4:8 filter is that it is a powerful tool for every spouse. No matter how much work you may think your spouse may need to do, how much improvement they could stand to make, the 4:8 filter shows us there is something worth celebrating. Look at the verse again.

> *Finally, brothers and sisters, whatever is true, whatever is noble, whatever is right, whatever is pure, whatever is lovely, whatever is admirable—if anything is excellent or praiseworthy—think about such things (Philippians 4:8 NIV).*

Did you catch that underlined word? *Anything.*

Anything?

If associating your spouse with words like noble, pure, and admirable is more of a stretch than you are willing to make, start instead with the word, *anything.* Is there *anything* excellent or praiseworthy about your spouse? Anything? I mean anything. Maybe they... have a job, take out the trash, wipe things, wipe children, talk to your Mom, hug you, root for the right team, floss, flush? Anything? *Start there.*

Start with one thing that is positive about them or something positive they did. Write it down, then each week add another thing to the list. Read the list every day for a couple of weeks. See what happens. I think you may be surprised what it *does to you and for you*—not to mention your spouse, and your Us.

One of my marriage expert heroes, the late Gary Smalley, often spoke about the honor book he kept about his wife, Norma. He had a journal in his desk drawer that listed out all the things he loved about his wife, which he added to often. He said whenever he was frustrated with her or needed to talk to her about something important, he would read through the honor book. He said this kept his head and his heart in a more loving place, which ultimately led to helping him handle situations in a more loving way. In other words, no one loses when we choose to see the best in our spouse. It's a win for everyone.

What Happens When We Try to See the Best in Our Spouse?

So, *how* exactly does seeing the best benefit both parties in our Us? Research says we are happier, more connected, more everything relationally good.[2] The apostle Paul says, peace. Right after the 4:8 filter, Paul writes in verse nine:

> *Whatever you have learned or received or heard from me, or seen in me—put it into practice. And the God of* ***peace*** *will be with you (NIV).*

Having peace when it comes to how you think about your spouse is no small thing. It's powerful. It makes relational deposits that pay off long term. One of the best examples of seeing the best that I have ever come across is from Debbie Wilkins Baisden. She describes what happened when she changed her mindset about marriage, in what is quite possibly the best marriage blog post in the history of marriage blog posts.

In *Stop Being A Butthole Wife,*[7] she shares her experience and how a change in mindset changed everything. I'm thrilled she graciously allowed me to share it below. She writes:

> *Stop being a butthole wife. No, I'm serious. End it. Let's start with the laundry angst. I get it, the guy can't find the hamper. It's maddening. It's insanity. Why, why, must he leave piles of clothes scattered, the same way that the toddler does, right? I mean, grow up and help out around here, man. There is no laundry fairy.*
>
> *What if that pile of laundry is a gift in disguise from a God you can't (yet) see? Don't roll your eyes, hear me out on this one. I was a butthole wife. Until my husband died.*
>
> *The day my husband left earth for Heaven, all of my marriage problems vanished. There was no one to fuss at, negotiate with, or play possum at bedtime (you know, when you pretend you're asleep to bypass sex).*
>
> *Marriage is designed to be a reflection of Christ's love for His people. It's supposed to be beautifully harmonious and intimate. How often I screwed that up with bickering and manipulating. I wanted a perfect husband who acted how I wanted, and if that didn't happen, well,*

butthole wife was in full effect. If only he could understand how right I was and how wrong he'd always be. I needed to instruct him, question him, and remind him of his shortcomings. After all, I was his "helpmate". The reality is, I wasn't helping him or our marriage. By pointing out each fault, I was poisoning the relationship. Oh, it was still a good marriage and we deeply loved each other, but it was not what it could have been. And now it was too late.

Days after his funeral, I stared at our dirty clothes basket that sat atop our dryer, knowing his clothes were inside. I sighed so deeply. Before me was the last load of laundry I would ever wash for that sweet man. There would be no more dirty socks to pick up around the house. Ever. A week before I would have rolled my eyes at that basket. But now, it held priceless treasures. I waited weeks to wash those clothes. My heart ached for dirty socks to once more be a part of my days. Those messes dotted around the house are reminders of God's gifts to us. Like Jesus, we have the opportunity to demonstrate love by serving those we live with. And the last time I checked, not a single person is perfect. How many times had my husband kept quiet, listened, and endured? He shared no list of ways that I needed refinement. He simply loved me. Those clothes were painfully cleaned and boxed away or donated. The tears countless.

But God, the Lover of my soul, in His infinite mercy, later gave me a special gift. He has allowed me to love again, to wear a second wedding dress, and to be a better wife.

I married a wonderful man. I am still a butthole wife, but I am working on edifying the man who provides for my sons and me. I now strive to hug more and nag less. My goal is to make him feel respected, important, valued. I want to live love.

Recently, I walked into the master bedroom and I stopped, nearly bursting into tears.

I saw a pile of dirty clothes that my new husband had abandoned on the floor. As I stared at the pile, I smiled. I knew he had hurried to change out of work clothes into comfy clothes so he could spend time with his new family. He had chosen what is more important. I happily scooped the treasures into my arms and carried them to the washing machine. I get to do this! I get to serve! I get to live with a wonderful man who ditches laundry for people.

I know this story is an extreme example—a story of someone experiencing tremendous loss before learning to be grateful for even the biggest annoyances. But the truth is, we can make the little annoyances our biggest pains. We tend to give these little annoyances far more weight and emotional energy than they deserve—and everyone around us suffers as a result. Believe me, I've been there. I get it. But no one wins when in that scenario. And I want you, I want your Us, to win. And there is nothing that can set you up to win more than seeing the best of your spouse. You can do this. You can see the best. When you do, you set up everybody, including yourself, to win. Constantly, consistently run your spouse through the Philippians 4:8 filter, and when you do, the reward is peace for you both.

Chapter Four

What Do You Think About Your Spouse's Emotions?

Do you ever have moments where you look at your spouse and think things like:

- I can't believe you just acted like that!
- I can't believe you got so upset about something so small!
- I can't believe that was such a big deal to you!
- I can't believe you are still mad about that, sad about that, celebrating that, laughing about that, talking about that!

Or maybe your spouse confuses you in different ways.

- Does your spouse get pumped up about Fantasy Football every year?
- Dances if your child gets a B instead of C?
- Celebrate a tidy garage more than your birthday?
- Laughs at shows that aren't funny?
- Thinks a sale at Target is God's modern-day equivalent to an Old Testament rainbow?

Fall Down Funny

In our marriage Nancie thinks I'm crazy because I find it funny when people trip and fall. Now, don't get me wrong, I don't want people to *break* anything in said fall, but if they *sprain* something? I think a sprain is a small price to pay for the joy it would bring me. Of course Nancie (and probably you at this point) thinks I'm crazy. She asks me, "How can you think that is funny? You are a pastor!" To which I tell her, "Exactly! I think God has a team of angels that trip people for my enjoyment." She is not convinced. Now, before you judge me—if you haven't already—I'm very generous with the joy that my own falls bring.

On a speaking trip in Dallas, I was on a run when I noticed the sidewalks were uneven. I remember thinking to myself, *"You better be careful, you could trip."* That thought was not even fully formed when the end of my shoe caught a bump in the sidewalk and tossed me forward. I tried to run it out. Is there anything better than watching someone trying to run it out? Turns out my attempt to run it out was unsuccessful. I slammed to the ground, scraping my hands and knees. I was bleeding. It hurt. My phone was cracked. But the first thought in my head was, "I really hope someone saw that." You know, because I'm generous like that. And just so you know, you couldn't possibly judge me for this personality trait more than Nancie already does.

I Just Don't Get It

The point is, sometimes we just don't get our spouse. We don't get what makes them happy, sad, or frustrated. Maybe your spouse has been frustrated with the same co-worker for ten years. Maybe your spouse feels defeated by peoples' Instagram pages. Maybe your spouse gets depressed around your family. Maybe your spouse acts as if other cars shouldn't be allowed on *their* road. Whatever it is, our spouse's emotions can leave us confused.

We wonder why they don't just get over it, get past it, move on, calm down—or why they don't tend to show any emotion at all! Their emotions can leave us wondering, frustrated, bewildered, devastated, discouraged, vulnerable, uncomfortable, and unsure of how to handle what *they* are feeling, making our spouse's emotions more about us than them.

As confusing as our spouse's emotions might be, how we handle them has far reaching implications. Turns out there is a correct way and a wrong way to do it. The wrong way often leads to disconnection and the right way often leads to connection. So, what's the secret? Empathy.

Empathy Defined

Empathy in marriage, as defined by leading marriage researcher John Gottman, is:

The capacity to identify and share someone else's emotions and experiences.[8]

Empathy has a radar to pick up what is going on with our spouse emotionally, and then steps into that emotion *with* them. That's why I love using Romans 12:15 as the definition of empathy. In this passage, the apostle Paul writes:

Rejoice with those who rejoice, cry with those who cry (NIV).

When it comes to empathy, the keyword is *with*. Rejoice *with* those who rejoice, weep *with* those who weep. It makes sense why this is such an important part in a marriage. Because on a very fundamental level, we get married to have someone to do life *with*. And that's exactly what happens in marriage. We are with our spouse through so much, everything from the day-to-day to the eventful. We are with them through finances, sex, children, work, moves, weddings, funerals, being richer, being poorer, experiencing sickness, experiencing health, walking through the better, and walking through the worse. ALL. THE. THINGS. From the mundane to mesmerizing we are *with* each other through all of it. And it's in the *with* that we find either great connection or great disconnection, all of which depends on how empathetic we are with our person.

Empathy Involves Fun. Who Knew?

There's another other word, I want to circle back to in Romans 12:15: *rejoice*. Most of the time we hear the word empathy we assume we need to be with someone who is sad. But empathy has just as much to do with celebration. In other words, empathy isn't just about the tough stuff in marriage, it's about the fun stuff.

Shelly Gable, professor of psychology at the University of California, Santa Barbara, discovered in her research, "How we *celebrate* is more predictive of strong relationships than how we fight." She states, "A partner's positive reaction to our good news can magnify the benefits of that good fortune and make us feel closer to them."[8] Of course it does! How we respond to their good news, to what excites them, really matters. We need to celebrate not just *for* them, but *with* them.

Sale-A-Bration

I've learned this over the years when it comes to my wife's ninja shopping skills. She is the queen of managing money. She carries around a bag of coupons with the same pride my grandmother did in the eighties. Some ladies strut around with Louis Vuitton, Nancie struts around with Ziploc™. All kidding aside, I'm very thankful for the way she manages our money. Consequently, I've learned to be present and celebrate what I call Sale Reveal Days.

Sale Reveal Days are when Nancie presents to me the great deals she has found. Recently, she came home with Old Navy bags and said, "Come with me." She took me to the bedroom. One by one, she took out each piece of clothing and laid them on the bed. "Look! I got five shirts, six pairs of shorts, five pairs of socks," ...etc. etc. "Guess how much I got all this for?" Now, you need to know that how I answer this question is crucial. I can't say, "I don't know, just tell me!" That is a joy killer. So, I have to guess a number that starts high, but not too high to be seen as condescending. In this case, I guessed $139. I could tell by her face this was a very good answer. While standing in her perfect Peter Pan stance, she said "Nope, lower." On the fly, I decided my guesses should go down in multiples of $10. I couldn't go too low too quickly because I needed to continue to be impressed by her epic score. Her face communicated that going down in multiples of $10 was also well-played. We played the game until we got to the number for a total cost of $36. I then asked the sincere question of, "How did you do that?" To which she explained how she combined an Old Navy sale, Old Navy dollars, (apparently, Old Navy has their own cryptocurrency), and a Pell Grant from the government to clothe our family for virtually zero dollars. Then I cue her for the final and most important part of the celebration, by asking, "How much *should* it have cost?" She said, "$38,754.00." Okay it wasn't that much, but it was close to $200 which was very impressive—to say the least. It was for sure worthy of celebration.

What Is Our Spouse Really Looking For?

So what was Nancie after emotionally in that moment? Was it about the clothes or was there something else going on? Bottomline, Nancie needed me to match her emotional excitement. She needed me to care by celebrating with her. This should be easy. And oftentimes it is easy because I'm so thankful for how she handles the finances for our family. (Plus, she is so stinking adorable and animated when she does her sale reveals, how could I not get excited for and more importantly, *with* her?!) She, in turn, graciously celebrates with me every time I cut the same lawn I've been cutting since 2006. I'm like a 6-year-old showing his mom a crayon drawing of a truck. When I'm finished with the lawn, I say, "Come outside with me." She stops what she is doing and walks outside with zero frustration. When she sees the lawn, she "oohs" and "ahhs" every time like it's the first time she's ever seen the ocean. Then I act like it is no big deal, and she goes on with a few more sentences of praise. The whole thing is pretty precious.

And let's be honest. Our marriages *need* precious, adorable, celebrations about temporary things. Life gets hard. Taking the time to celebrate cheap socks, cut grass, and other ridiculously average things isn't just a distraction, it's a necessity! It's what makes this marriage ride fun or not. I believe laughter, fun, and celebration are exactly what Paul was talking about in his letter to the Roman church. Because he knew there is power in coming alongside someone in their emotional experience. So, rejoice when your spouse rejoices, because rejoicing with your spouse reintroduces joy into the relationship. Be fun, be celebratory. You may be thinking, but I'm not that great at celebrating. That's okay! Make it a habit to practice, and work to get better at it. This is a zero risk proposition. You have nothing to lose and much to gain.

The Missing Link

Rejoicing with our spouse is one of the areas many of us are missing out on. I often see married people choosing the opposite. I see spouses responding to their spouse's excitement with rolled-eyes, disinterest, or outright contempt. Some spouses can be killjoys. And the thing is, there aren't many people who set out to be that way. No one stands at the altar on their wedding day promising to suck the life out of the person across from them. Even so, a few years down the road, a decade into marriage, and this can end up happening. We can stop rejoicing when our spouses rejoice. Why would we do that?

I think it could be for a lot of different reasons. And asking ourselves *why* we find it hard to rejoice with our spouse may be a helpful exercise. But I do know this. Researcher and author, Dr. Brené Brown has found that joy is the most vulnerable emotion.[10] There is something about expressing joy that can sometimes make us feel even more exposed than expressing sadness. But knowing how much vulnerability it takes to rejoice alongside a person we love, should give us hope. Imagine how much closer it could make you and your spouse if you allowed yourself to experience joy alongside them. Imagine what that might do for your relationship and the connection it could create.

If you are a few years out of practice, it may take some time to warm up to the idea. But give it a chance. Start small. If your spouse gets excited about their college team playing football. Don't be a killjoy. Don't comment on how much you hate football or how silly you think they are yelling at the tv. Put on a jersey and yell with them. If your spouse loves Christmas decorations a little too much, don't be a killjoy. Smile, notice, and enjoy decorations with them. Surprise them with matching ugly Christmas sweaters. If they get a promotion at work, celebrate via memes. Your phone is full of celebratory memes that will take you five seconds to text to your spouse. Take full advantage. Nancie and I believe memes are the 6th love language that everyone should speak. (Except our children, they think sending memes makes us dorks. That's okay, we think a lot of the things they do makes them dorks.)

The point is this. Marriage has enough tough stuff. Life can get serious. Have some serious fun and celebrate with your spouse. It's essential. As I stated in my book, Your Best US,[11] **one of the best ways to protect your marriage is to enjoy it.** Because when you don't celebrate with them, or when you belittle or ignore them, it hurts them and your Us. So why *wouldn't* you celebrate?

Now for the Tough Part

The second dynamic of empathy, or being with our spouses in their emotions, revolves around the tough stuff, or what Paul means when he writes to, *"cry with those who cry."* Some biblical translations of this verse use the word, *mourn.* Oftentimes, we aren't exactly sure what we want people to do when they come alongside us in our sadness or mourning—but when we experience someone doing it poorly, it becomes pretty obvious to us what shouldn't be said or done! Well-meaning people can say some hurtful things to someone who's grieving.

After my mom died, someone said to my grandmother—my mom's mom—"I don't know how you can do it. I couldn't stand to lose my daughter." Yikes! Some people also play these classics at funerals: "God Has A Plan," "They're in a Better Place," or "Everything Happens for a Reason." As a pastor, and as someone who has experienced a lot of personal grief, these words, as well-intentioned as they might be—often cause a lot more needless pain. People need our presence, not our platitudes. And that is at the heart of mourning with those who mourn. Because mourning with those who mourn means letting go of our tendency to want to fix, tie up in a bow, or make ourselves feel better for saying something spiritual. To mourn with those who mourn is to take our comfort out of the equation and elevate the well-being of the other person. And nothing we say or do can make right what has gone wrong. That is why we mourn. Because we can't fix it. We can't explain. We can simply be with them in their pain. And to be with them means it might hurt for us too.

I believe that also holds true with emotional pain in general. But somehow, Nancie and I missed that lesson in premarital counseling.
Oh wait, that's right, we never had premarital counseling. God bless our hearts.

My misunderstanding of Nancie's need for empathy caused much of the tension in our first few years of marriage. Our fights had the same steps, just different topics. They went as follows.

Step One: Nancie would share something bothering her.

Step Two: I tried to fix her problems with suggestions and encouragement.

Step Three: She argued why all my suggestions and encouragement were flawed.

Step Four: I got frustrated because I thought she didn't respect my opinions.

Step Five: The distance between us started to grow

Step Six: We were disconnected until one or both of us decided to let it go.

Feel Don't Fix

This happened over and over again in the early days. Then one day she said something to me that changed everything...when I allow it to. Don't miss this part. Please. It could be that this is as much of a turning point for your marriage as it was for ours. Nancie said to me, **"I don't want you to fix it, I want you to feel it."** She just wanted me to be *with* her. Let me say that again because it changed our marriage! "I don't want you to fix it, I want you to feel it." What does it look like to feel it with her? I will get to that, but I don't want you to miss the first part. "I don't want you to fix this."

In my defense—and in defense of all those who try to fix instead of feel—while fixing doesn't work, or isn't desired, it often comes from a good place. I adore Nancie and when I see her hurting, I want to help her. I don't want her to be in pain. I want to do everything I can to make it stop. But sometimes my motives are less selfless. **Sometimes the**

reason we try to fix our spouse's emotions is because we don't *like* their emotions. Because again, sometimes our spouse's emotions can be uncomfortable, unpleasant, inconvenient, or confusing to *us*. In other words, it's *possible* there are times we care more about being put out than about the pain our spouse is in. (I didn't say it was okay, I'm just saying, it's a reality.) Our spouse's unhappiness is inconvenient...to us. Their frustrations are uncomfortable...to us. So, to make our lives easier we try to rid ourselves of the angst by attempting to fix their problems. We give advice thinking maybe that will fix it. We ignore it. Maybe that will fix it. We argue why they shouldn't feel that way. Maybe that will fix it. For many of us, our Bob the Builder Relational Tool Box is full. Can we fix it? Yes, we can! But as Nancie so perfectly said, they don't need us to fix it, they need us to feel it.

Step in the Puddle

Turns out, Nancie's statement is backed by research. In the book, *How to Improve Your Marriage Without Talking About It,*[12] the authors reveal that most women want you to step into their emotional puddle, not yank them out of it. We see them standing in the emotional puddle, and we try to pull them out of it when what they really want us to do is step in the puddle. Now, I get that may sound super simplistic and over generalized. That may not describe every woman every time. And I know that there are many men who want to be joined in their emotional puddle as well. In fact, I remember my first counseling appointment. While I was tentative to go to see a counselor, once I was in his office, I just let go. I talked. I cried. And with all the things I had shared, I'm sure the counselor had a mountain of tremendously insightful things to say. Yet, he said almost nothing throughout the entire session. Instead, he stepped in the puddle with me. At the end of 50 minutes, he simply said, "You are really hurting." It was exactly what I needed to hear. My pain had been acknowledged with just four words. He knew I had zero capacity to hear anything more. I could not have handled nor would it have been effective for me to hear another syllable. I went on to see that counselor off and on for several years, and he helped me in so many ways. But he knew before I could hear any advice, I needed the profound gift of empathy.

In the same way, your spouse doesn't need you to fix it, they need you to feel it. **Your spouse is not a problem to be fixed, they are a person to be loved.**

Hold That Thought

You may be thinking, "But isn't honest, helpful advice needed, even essential?" Yes, but there is a time and place for it. And if your spouse is emotional, that is not the time or place for advice. In fact, if we get the timing wrong, we can end up making relational withdrawals, keeping our spouse from even hearing our advice—even if it's good advice! It can be good and helpful and still cause harm if the timing is off.

In fact, when your spouse is emotional, they are being driven by the emotional part of their brain. The logical part of their brain has greatly decreased in activity. So no matter how logical your advice, it won't matter because it will be received emotionally.[13] That's not necessarily a bad thing. In my experience, I have found **most of us give way too much weight to the power of our advice, and way too little to the power of empathy.** So choosing to be with them in their emotions isn't doing **nothing.** It's doing **something** really powerful. It's being empathetic and empathy is a relational connector.

Jesus showed us this time and time again. He shows us how understanding—really *getting* someone—can only be done up close. Religious leaders in Scripture kept a distance from the people Jesus made a beeline for. And it was when Jesus entered the world of the people the religious elite had stiff-armed, that Jesus was able to understand their uniquely painful world. It was His understanding that led to His empathy that led to His connection. A model for all of us. Empathy is worth the effort to get better at it.

That is why the intentional thought to memorize for this chapter is...

INTENTIONAL THOUGHT #3

⇨ "Choose Empathy."

When your spouse has a moment of excitement, say to yourself, "Choose empathy." When they get frustrated, angry, sad, say to yourself, "Choose empathy." When they are displaying an emotion for a reason you cannot understand at all, *choose empathy.*

To help you keep that in mind, I have something I think will help. When I looked for empathy exercises, I had a difficult time finding something I thought you and I would do. So, I want to give you something that I think we can all do—something you can say to yourself that will help you become more empathetic to your spouse's emotions. The next time your spouse is expressing frustration, feeling overwhelmed, articulating a problem—even if you think you have the best solution in the world to fix it, wrap it up, or move on, try thinking instead...

I See You. I Get You. I Got You.

Empathy is active. Empathy is letting your spouse know, I see you. I get you. I got you. That doesn't just happen. That requires an intentional move to get out of yourself for a minute and step into the puddle with your spouse. Now maybe you hear that and think, "But I need to DO something!" I get it. Believe me, I do. But here is the thing: pursuing empathy for your spouse IS doing something. Empathy is not passive.

I See You.

Our spouse needs to be seen figuratively *and literally.* Studies show simple eye contact produces empathy in you. That means, when you make eye contact with your spouse, it tends to create more empathy in *you,* for *them.* You can also mirror their emotions. Mirroring (not mocking) their emotions, means matching the look on their face with yours. When you mirror their emotions, it unlocks their mirroring neurons. Mirror neurons are the physiological foundation for empathy.[14] You mirroring their emotions, your eye-contact, brings the logical part of their brain back online. It helps them to feel less distress. When we see our spouse is in emotional distress, we want them to think more logically. But **your logic doesn't make them more logical, empathy does.**

In the same way, when your spouse is talking, especially if they are emotional, look at them. Don't roll your eyes at them, *fix* your eyes on them. Put down your phone and look at them. Look at their face. Watch their body language. To see them, you have to see what their face and body are communicating in addition to their words. Listen to their tone because their tone and volume are often more indicative of what is going on than their actual words.

My wife does an excellent job of reading between the lines with me. When I'm stressed about work, I can be a maximizer. I use the words: always, never, all, only, or nothing. But she knows my statements are often larger than I mean. "I can never get any work done at the library. I believe they have assembled a team of people whose only job is to distract me." Nancie sees me but doesn't try to fix me.

Many times, you can stop at, *I see you.* But sometimes you need to take it a step further to, *I get you.*

I Get You.

Our spouse needs to know we get them, which is why empathy is so powerful. It's the feeling of being understood. Perhaps that's one of the dynamics that brought you together in the first place. Maybe you said to your family and friends, "We just *get* each other." Often your spouse will feel you get them, by your non-judgmental, sincere, patient presence and nothing more is required. But, depending on how your spouse is wired, they may need you to verbally acknowledge that you understand the topic and the emotion. For instance, you say some things like,

- "You are frustrated at work because of the lack of teamwork. That's understandable."
- "You feel my mother overstepped with the kids and that makes you feel devalued as a mom."
- "You are discouraged with how our son is doing in school despite all the time you spent helping him with homework."

Your spouse needs to know you know. You don't just hear them. You don't just see them. You understand them.

It's also important to note empathy is not about understanding something from your point of view, but from someone else's. In other words, your job isn't to judge their emotions as right or wrong from where you are standing. It's to move out of your shoes and step into theirs. And experience them. Not dissect, talk out of, or rationalize them. Simply, experience. Along those lines, one sentence starter I have found to be helpful in moments where empathy is important is, "If I were you, I would feel the same way."

So, let's say your spouse is neater than you. They wake up to find a sink full of dirty dishes. They clean them, but they're frustrated they have to. You can say, "I apologize. If I were you, I would feel the same way." As yourself, you don't really care about the dishes. You aren't as neat. You aren't bothered. But your spouse does care. And if you were your spouse, you would care. That's empathy.

Regardless of the topic, they may need to hear you say, with no sarcasm or judgment things like:

- "I can see why this matters to you."
- "This hurt you. I hurt you."
- "The guy at work made you mad."
- "The lack of progress makes you frustrated."
- "I get it. If I were you, I would be upset too."
- "I get it. That is frustrating."

The point is, there may be no greater gift you can give your spouse than the gift of feeling understood. I think that's why the following statement has led to so much relational success for us over the past couple of years. Ready for it? *"That's understandable."*

Not long ago, on a Monday evening, following a full weekend of speaking seven times and traveling, Nancie asked me, "How are you doing?" She could tell something was off with me. I said, "To be honest, I'm tired and a bit depressed." All she said back, "That's understandable." It was balm to my soul. Sometimes she can try to cheer me up or even try to get to the root of why I'm feeling down, and to be honest, a lot of times that can take more emotional energy than I have to give. "That's understandable" was exactly what I needed.

Wait a Minute

You may be wondering, "What if what they are feeling is not understandable to me? What if I think they are being anywhere from slightly-off to outrageous? What if I don't agree with them on the topic or issue they are being emotional about? What if we are fighting about what they are emotional about?"

These are great questions. And I understand them. Because oftentimes we confuse empathy with agreement. We think to have empathy we are endorsing their opinions and feelings and co-signing. But validating and agreeing are two different things. If your spouse is mad you are late and you think they are overreacting, you don't have to agree. Simply say, "My being late frustrated you. I'm sorry." Often, once your spouse knows you understand and have validated what they are experiencing, empathy has done its job. But depending on your spouse and the situation, you may want to consider one final step: *I got you.*

I Got You.

This is when you leverage what you *get* about them to let them know you *got* them. This is the part where you ensure your spouse knows you have their back. Often this means you do nothing further than letting them know *you see* them and *you get* them. Other times, it means you should do something. Maybe they need you to pick up the slack around the house. They need you to tell the kids to knock it off. They need you to say you're sorry. They need you to celebrate over dinner. Or they need you to do the happy dance. Maybe they need you to send them a text celebrating or commiserating. The point is, "I got you" is communicating what you are willing to *do* to help them feel understood.

Oftentimes we think this will involve doing something *more*. But sometimes communicating you got them, begins with *stopping* something. In fact, in marriage, stopping things is often as important as starting things. One of the greatest ways to show your spouse empathy is to change the behavior that is causing them emotional distress, even if you don't understand it—*especially* if you don't understand it. If they are frustrated about you being late, stop being late. If rolling your eyes about their mother hurts them, stop rolling your eyes. If shouting at people in traffic stresses them out, stop shouting at people in traffic.

When we were first married, sometimes I would be demonstrative with my frustrations with other people and situations. In my mid-to late twenties, when I was frustrated with someone other than Nancie, it wasn't beneath me to slam my fist down or growl. One night she was frustrated with me for doing that, and I said, "Why do you care? I'm not mad at you." She said, "I don't want to be in the room with it." There you have it. And now, with some maturity, that makes 100% sense. Why would anyone want to be in a room with a man acting like a toddler? And even if I didn't understand why she didn't like it, empathy requires that I love her by keeping that sort of thing to myself. "I got you" in this context meant stopping a behavior, because it was the most loving thing to do for her.

The More You Know

As if these weren't already enough reasons to lean into empathy in your marriage, another reason empathy is so powerful is because it helps you to know your spouse better. Empathy requires us to be aware of what is going on with our spouse and be curious about *why*. Empathy informs us about what makes our spouse happy, sad, mad, frustrated, and everything in between. And this matters because the more you know your spouse, the better you can love them. By getting insight into what makes your spouse who they are, you are more equipped to empathize with them when they need it most. It may not come naturally, but the more you practice it, the more natural it will become.

When Helen Fisher studied the brains of happily married people, she found there were high levels of activity in the part of the brain that is responsible for empathy.[2] Whether these couples' brains were wired this way from birth, or they learned it along the way, the end result is the same: more empathy. So if empathy feels nearly impossible to demonstrate right now, take heart. You aren't a lost cause! We can train our brains to have more empathy. It starts with: I see you, I get you, I got you.

Look at That!

Marriage researcher Dr. John Gottman has found that couples who are happy, understand this. Dr. Gottman says that married people make *bids* towards each other for connection. He defines bids for connection as **any attempt from one partner to another for attention, affirmation, affection, or any other positive connection.**[15]

Bids show up in simple ways—a smile or wink—and more complex ways—like a request for advice or help. He reports that couples who are happy, accept their partner's bids *three times more* than couples who report being unhappy. If your spouse says, "Look at that!" *Look.* They want to share something with you.

When All Else Fails

If your marriage is in a tough season, empathy may be even more crucial. Why? I think Erwin McManus says it best in his book *The Genius of Jesus,* where he writes, "Empathy is the path to ending the divide between us and the only hope for pulling us together." That was certainly true of our friends—I'll call them Sam and Beth—who have allowed me to share their story.

About six years ago, Sam made some choices that would have justified Beth seeking a divorce. They attempted counseling for over a year and a half to focus on those behaviors. They focused on changing and monitoring those behaviors, with no success, until both of them felt done with their marriage. But they have four children, and because of them, they decided to give it one last try. For a last-ditch effort, they attended a 4-day marriage intensive at a marriage retreat center. This marriage intensive focused on the emotions and the cause of behaviors. Both Sam and Beth were asked to focus on the root cause of Sam's choices which they determined was childhood abuse. Directed to sit face to face, looking at one another, Beth was asked to focus on Sam when he was a boy. She was asked to focus on the hurt, the pain, and the emotions of that little boy, and to empathize with Sam who had carried that weight his entire life. Beth said she could not *relate* to the pain, but she could *empathize* with a hurting soul. She saw a soul that was trying to do what was right, what was honoring, but that had so many obstacles because of so much trauma.

Beth said it was shifting her mindset from being wronged, to a mindset of empathy and compassion that gave the slightest bit of hope for their marriage. Sam still had work to change his behaviors for the marriage to work, but empathy opened up a road to healing. Beth's choice to empathize softened her stance. Sam was asked to do the same exercise for Beth. He was asked to empathize with the little girl in the woman sitting in front of him. He was asked to empathize with the triggering his actions caused for that little girl inside the woman in front of him.

He saw the pain he had caused with an even deeper sense of empathy. And in this incredibly intimate practice, a way forward for their marriage was made possible.

Maybe the idea of doing this with your spouse sounds like a form of torture; like it requires an emotional vulnerability that feels next to impossible to demonstrate. I get it. Remember, this was a four day marriage intensive. This sort of thing isn't for the faint of heart. And yet, as deeply uncomfortable as it may have been or as it may sound to you, it offered a breakthrough for Sam and Beth.

When I was interviewing Beth for this book, she said, "I do not want someone to mistake my action of empathy to mean everything was immediately okay after that or that I just turned a blind eye. What I would like for them to hear is that empathy opened up a door to healing. Lots of work took place after that moment at the marriage intensive but our hearts were more connected, were softened to each other, and more open to healing. We saw each other as broken people trying to honor each other and our marriage."

It was that empathy that gave her back hope and heart for their marriage. Beth and Sam have been pouring into their marriage ever since. As Beth told me it hasn't always been easy or perfect, but they are closer than ever because they chose to stay *with* each other—but more than that, they chose to do the work necessary to create their best Us. Had they not, they either would have gotten divorced or stayed together in name only, robbing themselves and their children of participating in and witnessing the fruits of a well-fought for and tended to marriage. In other words, they knew a win for them was not leaving, but also not just simply staying. It was changing the way they approached their marriage, saw each other and thought about each other. As a result of their personal experience, Beth now has a ministry to help other women navigate similar situations. And her brave, vulnerable, choice of empathy was the start of it all.

Where Do You Need to Have More Empathy with Your Spouse?

What about you? Where do you need to have more empathy with your spouse? What is the area where they have tension or discomfort and what is their emotion? Is your spouse: grieving the loss of a parent, frustrated with an illness, worried about money, grieving a child moving to college, anxious about being a new parent? Practice the steps we've walked through. Practice saying: *I see you. I get you. I got you.* Practice thinking to yourself, *choose empathy.* You will not regret it.

Opening and Closing Doors

Sam and Beth were an example of a marriage facing some huge hurdles. But sometimes, it's the little, day-to-day stuff that can also create big tensions—and the most opportunity to practice empathy. Our newly married friend, Kellen taught us a powerful lesson about this very thing. Kellen is a self-described neat freak. Recently his wife, Katie, didn't shut the laundry room door. Kellen said the door is "wonky" and you have to shut it a certain way or it comes back open. He said he knew he wouldn't be comfortable until he shut it. So he shut it and Katie said, "Sorry," for not doing it. But Kellen responded by saying, "I don't mind shutting it, as long as you don't mind me shutting it. I realize this is my thing, not yours."

Kellen and Katie's story is about such a small thing—but something that still required self-awareness and empathy to resolve. Think about it. Kellen could have said, "Katie, can you just shut the door? It takes two seconds. You know it drives me crazy." And Katie could have responded with, "If you want it shut, you shut it. It doesn't bother me that it's open. How silly can you be?"

If they had chosen the latter way, how do you think it would have impacted the rest of their day? We all know it would not have gone well—probably because we have all experienced days where that was the approach we took and as a result, the day was ruined! This story of Kellen and Katie was the one story Nancie suggested I include in this book. She said—and I quote—"Kellen and Katie's story says so much. There is something powerful about saying, "I know there are things about me that are hard to be married to." You preach it, Nancie Lowe! And I just want to say in print, I know there is a lot about me that's hard to be married to. Perhaps nothing leads to greater empathy than a self-awareness of our own annoying habits—like forgetfulness, stubbornness, procrastination, pettiness, things having to be a certain way. In other words, a self-awareness of where we don't always get it right and see our own humanity can allow us to empathize more with our spouse. **When we are aware of the places we fall short, we can see the places our spouse falls short with much more grace and understanding.**

Small Things Are Big Deal

Shutting doors and sales at Old Navy matter to your marriage, because the little things add up. Small moments of seeing your spouse and attempts to understand your spouse lay the groundwork for empathizing with your spouse. And best of all? *Empathy isn't complicated.* Perhaps the most beautiful thing about it is its simplicity. You don't need a graduate degree or doctorate. You don't need to be a psychologist or a counselor. You just need to be a student of your spouse. Rejoice when they rejoice. Mourn when they mourn. Practice presence with them and watch your marriage begin to change.

Empathy is the start of hope and the protector of close connections. Now it's your turn. Make your goal to have the following conversation with your spouse within the next week. My hope for you is that you would make it a weekly ritual.

Think About It

Get with your spouse and ask the following High/Low questions:

High

I see you: What is one thing you need me to celebrate?

I get you: What makes this special to you?

I got you: How can I celebrate with you?

Low

I see you: What is one thing that is concerning you?

I get you: What makes it troubling?

I got you: How can I let you know I have your back?

Chapter Five

What Do I Think About My Response?

LET ME ASK YOU A DANGEROUS QUESTION, but when I ask you, don't say your answer out loud to your spouse, don't look at your spouse, don't elbow them, and don't make that noise you make when they frustrate you. Just *don't*. Okay, are you ready? Here's the question: **What is that thing your spouse does that triggers you?** You may have an immediate answer. Or you may need to think through it a bit more. Here are a few typical triggering areas: money, sex, parenting, communication, chores, emotions, or the biggest marital issue in North America: how to load a dishwasher.

No matter where in the country I am speaking, I know if I want to get a strong reaction from the audience, I simply have to say the word, dishwasher. And I get it. The dishwasher has been a thing between Nancie and me for years. Turns out there are two types of people (only one of which I understand). Group 1 believes you can put in as many dishes as you want, any way you want, as long as the dishwasher door can close enough to start. I belong to this group, and though this doesn't need to be said, we are the spiritual people. Group 2, God bless your souls, believes there is a "way" to load a dishwasher. First you pre-rinse, then you place the dishes in a certain fashion/direction. This group also believes if their spouse doesn't choose the correct "way," they must take it upon themselves to reload the correct "way." My wife, unfortunately, belongs in this group.

Yes, in the little things and the big things our spouse can trigger us. And this shouldn't come as a surprise, because of how intertwined our lives are with our spouse's. Almost everything our spouse does impacts us individually. The way they handle chores, emotions, communication, and frustrations, can all radically impact our lives. So, when our spouse does something frustrating, hurtful, "wrong," it triggers us. And it is so easy, even natural, to react without thinking. To make matters even worse: there is usually little to no time between what triggers us and our reaction to that trigger. There's a *reason* why it is so easy to get into conflict when we are triggered.

What's Going On in That Head of Yours

Let's unpack that a bit. The set of structures in your brain called the limbic system is where emotions begin. In the limbic system is our culprit: the amygdala. Now, in its defense, the amygdala *is* super helpful. The amygdala is responsible for sending us alerts letting us know when we aren't safe. These alerts result in us taking steps to protect ourselves. So, the amygdala is a great thing. It's the part of our brain that makes us take our hand off a hot stove without having to think about it. We don't have to stop and say, "Ouch, this is hurting like what I assume to be the second level of Hades, so I will remove my hand to stop said pain." No. Our amygdala is automatic, which serves us well when we need to protect ourselves from things like stoves, buses, wild boar, and politics. And it's the amygdala that is triggered by our spouse when we face conflict.

Fight, Flight, or Freeze?

When it comes to marriage, the amygdala is too efficient, leading us to often react *before* thinking. When the amygdala is triggered, people typically tend to react in one of three ways: fight, flight, or freeze. If fighting is your thing, then when you are triggered, you tend to step *toward* the tension. You quickly say something with your words and/or your body language to let your spouse know you are not okay with what just happened. If your thing is flight, then you typically step *away* from the tension. Your response involves finding ways to escape the situation. You withdraw emotionally and/or physically. The final response is freezing. You don't know what to say or what to do, so you do nothing. You don't step toward or away from the tension, you simply *stay put.*

Whether you are a fighter, flee-er, or freezer, your amygdala reacts before consulting the part of the brain responsible for thought and judgment—which is called the cortex. This is the part of the brain that thinks and remembers logically that: getting angry doesn't work and issues are never resolved by fighting. It's the part of our brain that knows hurting your spouse with your words will not change their behavior. In fact, it often does the opposite. Our amygdala reacts before our cortex considers the consequences. And our automatic responses may not always be the best ones.

The problem is, it is *so* easy to be triggered, because we are so different from one another. For example; sometimes really neat tidy people—people who want everything lined up perfectly—people who believe everything has a place and everything should be in its place—sometimes those types of people marry normal people. My wife is so neat our junk drawer has dividers, which I try to tell her makes it by its very essence, not a junk drawer.

Or sometimes savers marry spenders and the savers rob joy from the spenders. That is how that works. For instance, when I go to Home Depot for lightbulbs, and come back with a riding lawn mower, for some reason, it triggers Nancie.

Because married life is so intertwined, we have many opportunities to trigger each other. But again, the trigger in and of itself isn't the problem.

It's how we react without thinking after we are triggered. We are hardwired to react immediately, and while this doesn't excuse our bad reactions, it does help explain them. It explains why people who really want to be a good spouse, find themselves doing and saying *again*, that thing they promised they would never do or say again.

Better Than Understanding the Problem

Understanding what is going on in your brain during tension is a good thing to know—but I am not sure it's common knowledge. It wasn't for me until a few years ago because nobody tells you this stuff. But once I learned it, it was so transformative for our marriage, I had to share it. Because what is even more powerful than knowing *why* something isn't working, is knowing *how* to fix it.

Based on the wiring of our brains, I want to give you two quick verses that tell us exactly what to do when we are triggered, found in James 1:19–20. Again, even if you aren't sure how you feel about the Bible speaking into your marriage, be assured this verse makes what is validated by scientific research very practical. And if you, like me, are a follower of Jesus, taking these verses seriously isn't optional.

To set the stage, I want you to imagine, your spouse has just triggered you. Now imagine pausing the scene.

It's in this pause that James, the brother of Jesus, instructs us what to do.

> *My dear brothers and sisters, take note of this:*

James was speaking to new Jesus followers, who he wanted to have right relationships. In other words, whatever he is about to say, he is saying it out of love. He continues...

> *Everyone should be quick to listen, slow to speak, and slow to become angry, (James 1:19 NIV).*

This verse gives us very specific instructions on how to pause, and I will unpack each of those ways, but first let's acknowledge why pausing is so crucial. When we are triggered, it takes six to eight seconds for the amygdala to relax enough to get us back to a calm space. (Eight seconds is also the amount of time a bull rider has to stay on in order to be scored, which has nothing to do with what I'm talking about; it's just a really cool stat.)

Eight seconds is the length of the pause you need, *but,* get this, studies show that with practice, the time needed to let the amygdala calm down can *shorten* as you practice pausing. We can improve our pausing with practice.

Let's review a bit,

The natural order of things is

Trigger — Reaction

Using James' advice, there is a supernatural order of things which is...

Trigger ——— Pause ——— Response

This space after being triggered is where relationships are built or broken.

In fact, one study showed that 96% of the time, how your partner will respond in a conversation—whether that's positive or negative—will depend on the attitude you have at the start of a conversation. That attitude is directly related to whether or not we are allowing our amygdala or our cortex to call the shots. The great news is, we can choose a response, instead of just submitting to or relying on our automatic response, which may or may not be our best one.

Repair Attempts

This all sounds great. But let's be honest. It is so easy *not* to pause, and just barrel ahead causing damage we never intended. So, what about those times when we react before thinking? Is it too late? It doesn't have to be. Studies show that couples with the highest level of marital satisfaction have a tool they use during those situations. In other words, even if we have missed the chance to get it right the first time, not all hope is lost! We can get back on track with what Dr. John Gottman calls a repair attempt. He defines a **repair attempt** as **"any statement or action—silly or otherwise—that prevents negativity from escalating out of control."**[16]

A repair attempt is something happy couples use to keep things from going sour in the first place, or from more sour than they already are. When one or both of them feel triggered, they do something to pause. Most couples who use repair attempts don't know the term or intentionally choose it, it is just something they happen to do naturally. But those of us who don't implement repair attempts naturally, can learn to. Repair attempts can be as simple as saying:

- Let me press pause. Can I redo that?
- Let me press pause. I'm sorry, I can tell I just hurt you.
- Let me press pause. This isn't your problem; this is our problem.
- Let's press pause. We are on the same team here.
- Let's press pause. I'm getting defensive, can you say that in a different way?
- Let's press pause. I need a break, but I promise to come back when I can talk about it calmly.

Our spouse needs an attempt from us to let them know we are not trying to attack them. They need to know we are safe. Whatever your pause is, you need to plan your pause when you are calm, because in the heat of the argument, we can't count on our rational thinking to remember to pause. Perhaps there is no time like the present.

Hopefully, you aren't currently worked up about anything, which makes now a great time to plan your calm response. So, take a minute and ask yourself: **What is something you can do or say to slow things down when you are triggered?**

....

....

....

....

Breaking It Down

James gives us really specific pointers on how to learn to pause. These are not sequential steps to follow, but things happening simultaneously.

Here's what James says:

1. Be Quick to Listen.

When we are triggered, it is natural to immediately stop listening, start talking, and defend ourselves. Hearing what our spouse is trying to tell us is low on our priority list. But by pausing, we have a better chance of seeing what is truly hurting them and of learning how to get out of our perspective and into theirs.

That doesn't mean they may not be wrong or hurtful in what they are saying or doing, but it does mean we have a better chance of getting on the same page sooner. I'll be honest, if I think Nancie has said something "big," wrong, or hurtful in the course of a disagreement, pausing is not easy for me. This is because I love words. Words are a big deal to me, and a huge part of my life. Nancie has a harder time putting her words together. She once said to me, "When you are angry you find your words. When I'm angry I lose mine." When she is trying to find them, sometimes she can say things in a way she doesn't intend. This is where I need to practice a huge amount of grace. (And by the way, often the words I so quickly find when I'm angry are not always the best ones for our marriage.)

Plus, I need to remember, *we* need to remember, our spouse's frustrations speak to something that matters to them, something that goes deeper than their angry words might communicate. Anger and frustration are often a front to an underlying hurt, fear, or vulnerability. Their words and tone may be saying one thing, but as someone who loves them, it is our job to go one layer deeper. And when we pause, we make time to ask: Is it possible there is more going on here than I can see right now? This type of pause gives us a better chance of achieving a healthier relationship in the long run, and avoiding some relational pitfalls in the short run.

And again, this is a great space to give our spouse grace. Most of us weren't taught relationship skills growing up. We weren't instructed how to *do* marriage. And neither was our spouse! So give them grace, and try to understand what they are *really* trying to say. Maybe you've never completely heard them on this specific issue. Or maybe you think you fully understand their opinion on this issue. But maybe, just *maybe*, you don't. Maybe there is just one piece of information or hurt you don't understand. Listening again is never a bad idea.

The Part He Didn't Know

I saw an amazing illustration of this while creating a small group video series. In this particular series, I told couples I would be interviewing them. But right when the director said action, I said, "So I've decided not to interview you. Actually, I'm leaving and I'm going to let you interview each other." I left them with questions on cue cards. I instructed them to allow their spouse to answer and offer little comment in return. I assured them they would get their turn when their spouse asked them the same questions.

Michael and Shameka were interviewing each other and the conversation went a bit like this: She asked him, "How can I make our home a better place?" He said, "When I come home at night, I just need a few minutes before you and the kids start talking to me. There are times I'm not even in the door and you are asking me questions about the next day. I have to talk to people all day. So, when I get home, I need a moment to unwind."

Shamika remained calm, but you could tell in her eyes and by her body language that she had been triggered. You could see it in her eyes and body language. When it was Michael's turn to interview Shamika, he started with the same questions. When he asked, "How can I make our home a better place?" she said calmly, "When you come home from work, you seem frustrated to see us. Everywhere you go you are talking—at work, at church, even with strangers. Then when you get home, you often tell the kids and me that you don't have any more words. That hurts. The reason I ask you questions about the next day is that it is typically late when you come home, and I need the answers to make the next day work for our family." He seemed taken aback, but he simply nodded telling her he understood what she was saying. Then the cameras turned off and he said to her "Oh honey, I never knew you felt that way! I don't know how I missed it. I'm so sorry."

This is a great example of what couples can talk about when they aren't mad, and of the progress we can make when we don't respond reactively. **So many married people only talk about frustrating things in the middle of frustrating things.** They sabotage the conversation from the very start! They only talk about money when they are frustrated about a surprise purchase on the credit card bill. They only talk about chores when someone has left a mess. They only talk about sex when the offer has been declined. But when couples' brains and bodies are calm, they can talk and—more importantly—they can listen.

Michael, the husband from the story I just shared, is not a bad man. Actually, I intentionally invited him to be a part of the video series because he is an extraordinary man. It might be easy to write him off as clueless or insensitive, but the truth is, he is a lot like us. He had no ill intent towards his wife. He just missed it. His brain and his body weren't on his side when he was triggered by his wife's questions, and he didn't know it. He had been taught how to do his job, but not how to be a husband. Now he knows. Now he can make a different choice. Now he understands to listen when there is tension. And we can too.

I watch countless couples at marriage retreats and events have effective conversations about tough things *because they aren't in the middle of those things.* And that is because their bodies and brains are set up to win. They have inserted a pause that gives them the ability to discover how to love each other better.

Now, back to James.

2. Be Slow to Speak.

I really believe if you get this next part right, it could revolutionize your relationship. This could be the thing you have been needing to do for 30 years. In fact, married people say to me all the time, "Just tell me what to do!" And I respond by giving them this one piece of advice, especially when it comes to conflict. I say to them—and to you and me: *When you are triggered, don't talk.* Don't say anything negative with your words or with your body language.

While researchers debate on the percentages, there is no debate around the fact that much of communication is non-verbal.[17] So while pausing and not talking is crucial once triggered in an argument, so is paying close attention to what our bodies may be saying. In other words, nonverbal communication matters just as much. We don't have to open our mouths to communicate frustration, anger, or contempt. We simply have to cross our arms, roll our eyes, set our jaw, and bore holes into our spouse's forehead with an angry glare. In the same way, we don't have to open our mouths to communicate love, compassion, and understanding. Depending on your person, you can make intentional caring eye contact, take a step closer, or offer a reassuring touch.

Maybe all of this sounds overly simplistic, but the truth is, I believe people like me, whose full-time job is to focus on marriage, tend to over-complicate things. And this doesn't have to be complicated. When you are triggered, at first, do not talk. It's that simple.

Brené Brown, behavioral researcher, goes as far as to say that **when you are shamed, you shouldn't talk, text, or type until you allow the logical part of your brain to come back online.**[18] Don't address the situation until you have time to become calmer *and* to remember what you want for your relationship—not just what will serve as an emotional release in the moment.

One of the most powerful parts of pausing is that it will lead to a response versus a reaction. A response is intentional. A reaction is automatic. If we want to avoid regret in high conflict moments, responses, not reactions, are key! So the next time you are triggered, imagine me waving my arms, shouting, "DON'T TALK." But it doesn't have to be me. You can imagine a bear, SpongeBob, Mickey Mouse, or Dr. Phil. No matter what the mental cue, just remember, when you are triggered, at first *just don't talk.* Don't talk with your words, your face, or your body.

The last thing James tells us is:

3. Be Slow to Become Angry.

It's not enough to just tell ourselves, "Don't be angry". We need to get specific and ask ourselves: What does anger or frustration look like on me? How do I respond when I am triggered? Am I loud? Passive-aggressive? Distant? Demonstrative? Sarcastic? Maybe even ask your spouse how they perceive you when you get angry. Know your signs when an emotional trigger sets you off, so you can be better prepared to stop anger from calling the shots.

It must be said, anger is a normal emotion for all of us. But when we express it inappropriately, it almost always leads to things going sideways in our marriages. Anger complicates the issue. It doesn't resolve it. Anger handled improperly leads to distance and pain. Which is why I think it's so important to pay attention to the word James uses right before anger: *become.*

Pausing is so important because with no effort at all, we can allow our anger to shape us into a version of ourselves our spouse deserves better than. You don't want to *become* the spouse you don't want to be. You don't want to *become* the spouse who says whatever they want or who acts however they want when they are angry. That is what we did when we were children. And I can tell you from experience, I can handle anger like a child! But we are all big people now and we can make better choices. We can't afford not to!

Of all the points made in this book, this is one of the biggest. I want you to know and live out your ability to *choose* how you respond to your spouse. I want that for you because this has been one of the best things I have learned and then implemented in our marriage.

Part of having ADHD is the struggle with impulse control. Growing up, my parents and teachers often asked me after I did something I shouldn't, "What were you thinking?" But that was the problem. I didn't think before I acted! I just acted! This lasted long into adulthood. But I have discovered that even I can learn to pause long enough to have a better response. We all can.

All of us are capable of choosing a response versus a reaction out of anger. We can choose to pause. We can choose to listen, not speak, and to control our anger. As temperament expert Kathleen Edelman says, "You choose the words you use." Yes, *you can choose.*

What Fills The Pause?

Okay, so we get that the pause is important. But the next question becomes, what do we do with the pause? What fills that space?

You could do any number of things and it can last any amount of time. For some of us, that pause will need to last eight seconds. For others of us, eight minutes will do the trick. For some of you eight hours or longer might be necessary. The amount of time you need will help determine how you spend that pause.

There are a lot of things you can do here, and it might be helpful for you to keep a running list of things that work for you. For some people a pause is best filled by getting some air, taking a walk, or doing some other sort of physical exercise to **get your cortex on line and your amygdala in line.** Other people find that engaging in some deep, measured breathing helps. Sitting with your eyes closed, inhaling for three seconds, holding your breath, and then exhaling for three seconds can work wonders in calming down your fight, flight, or freeze reflex.

Others have found prayer to be a helpful way to fill the pause. Inviting God into this space is a way to tap into the Holy Spirit to help guide your words and actions.

If the idea of praying in that pause feels hyper-spiritual, you can rest easy. I'm not talking about fancy prayers, I'm talking about super simple and straightforward prayers like "Help me, Jesus!" "God, would You please help me to love well right now?" Or my favorite, "God, please make space for grace." However you choose to fill the pause, the point is the same: you will be better for it. I've experienced it first hand—if anyone needed to learn the benefit of pausing, it was me.

The Art of Saying the Wrong Thing

Growing up, I learned the unfortunate art of how to verbally defend myself, and not in a good way. If I felt threatened, attacked, or put on the defensive, I could verbally fight back with the best of them. It was actually pretty impressive, if I do say so myself. The problem is, I took this skill into my marriage. I was shocked at how quickly I could respond to Nancie in frustration, and I knew I didn't want that for our family. So, over the years, through prayer, wise counsel, and other resources, I learned to pause, be quicker to listen, slower to speak, and slower to become angry. Do I get it perfect every time? No. But now I have a why and a how-to pause, and more importantly, I have learned the power of a simple prayer: God, please make space for grace.

You can choose to do the same; it is possible for everyone. You may be like me and need a counselor's help—there's no shame in that. But it doesn't have to be a counselor. It can be a friend, mentor, pastor, or coach. Just make sure this person is for your marriage **and** your spouse, not just you. But make no mistake about it, if you want to get great at pausing, having great people on your team makes it so much easier. We all need people in our lives who want our marriage to win.

I'll Be Back

Yes, there are huge payoffs from pausing. But we can't talk about pausing without also emphasizing the importance of *coming back*. A pause isn't about running away and hoping things resolve themselves on their own. You have to come back with a response—not a reaction—that has been thought through and/or prayed about, that is used to draw you back together, not create more distance. A well utilized pause allows you to come back and ask better questions and talk in a healthier way with one another, in a way that gives space and grace.

Or you may find in your pause that you don't need to say anything at all. In fact, often a pause gives you what you need to jumpstart the forgiveness process. You can simply say to yourself:

"I don't need to bring this up again, I was just tired."

"I don't need to bring this up, this is my issue, not theirs."

"I don't need to bring this up, they don't have the emotional capacity to deal with it right now."

"I don't need to bring this up because it simply does not matter."

"I don't need to bring this up because we are wired differently and we are always going to see this differently."

"I can decide to keep no record of wrong."

Responding this way is not sweeping conflict or tension under the rug. It's inviting grace into the conversation and using wisdom to discern what is a conversation worth engaging in and when. I'm talking about pausing to communicate in a way that leads to *connection*.

That is why the **intentional thought** I want you to memorize from this chapter is simply this:

INTENTIONAL THOUGHT #4

⇨ "Pause."

The next time you are triggered, say to yourself, "Pause." And then, actually do it! You are capable of inserting that simple break—however long it needs to be—to keep conflict and tension from owning you. Then, be quick to listen, slow to speak, and slow to become angry. This isn't *easy*, but it certainly makes your life *easier*, because when you practice pausing there is less relational clean-up.

Isn't it true that some of the biggest regrets in our marriages are the things we wished we hadn't said? But when we pause long enough to love and to be slow to speak, we live life with fewer of those regrets. Because the truth is, you can always say something more, but you can never unsay something. **So while saying you're sorry is great, not needing to say sorry is better.**

This principle is found all over Scripture. Proverbs 18:21 says, *"The tongue has the power of life and death" (NIV).* That may sound like an exaggeration, but chances are, we have experienced the truth of this proverb firsthand. We know both the good and the harm words can cause. And if this is true, if words are a matter of life or death, then at the very least, it makes sense to pause and consider them. **Because pausing leads to better responses and better responses lead to better marriages.**

The Big Why

Finally, James not only gives us very practical wisdom to know **how to pause,** he gives us the **why**. Let's go back to what James wrote., *"Be quick to listen, slow to speak, and slow to become angry, **because** anger does not bring about the righteous life God desires" (James 1:19 NIV).*

Righteousness is just another way of saying right living. It's about doing relationships right. It's about having the relationship God desires for you to have. And I believe God hardwired into the core of us that same desire—to do marriage in a way where our relationship becomes a place of grace, compassion, laughter, and intimacy. That relationship is built, in part, by implementing the difficult—yet simple—*pause*.

Look, you know this already. But learning to pause in the midst of conflict can be a game-changer for your marriage. And chances are, there are a lot of us who need something to change in our marriage. Maybe we haven't been able to articulate what or know how, but we know the marriage we want is not the marriage we have. And if we are to have the marriage we want, we may do well to lean into the third and final revelation from Dr. Helen Fisher's study on the brains of long-term couples who are madly in love. That revelation: controlled emotions. Couples in love seem to have a brain wired to keep their emotions in check. While our brains may be wired differently, we are not at a loss. We just have to try, try, again.

So, what if, the next time you get triggered, you try something different by practicing a pause? If you are really struggling in your marriage, take heart: the more tension you are having as a couple, the more opportunities you have to get good at pausing. And eventually, with practice, **it's possible to become a pro at not letting silly fights lead to serious damage.** If you have kids, they can grow up seeing you model a healthy way of handling conflict. Imagine if you looked back on this time and said, "This was a time we got closer because I learned how to love better, simply by learning to pause." *That* would be the start of a new day in your marriage.

This week, and hopefully way beyond, when you see the pause symbol, when you use a pause button, remember that pausing is what happy couples do and any couple can learn. You got this. Be quick to listen, slow to speak, and slow to anger. Be quick to pause. To help you practice pausing, do the exercise below. You will be glad you did.

Think About It

Imagine you are triggered. Now list how you can...

Be Quick to Listen

Slow to Speak

Slow to Become Angry

Chapter Six

What Do You Think Is the Purpose of Your Us?

HAVE YOU EVER HAD MARRIAGE MOMENTS, even seasons when you were thinking, “What is all *this* about?”

Maybe you are newly married and reality doesn’t remotely resemble what you were expecting. He or she is not acting, smelling, or picking up their clothes in the way you hoped and they promised. You may be asking, what is all *this* about?

Or maybe it's the opposite. You are newly married and shocked why people say the first year is the toughest. You are doing great. What is all *this* about?

Maybe you are trying to get pregnant and month after month you are disappointed. Meanwhile, you can't go on social media for two minutes without seeing another gender reveal. What is all *this* about?

Or maybe you are one of the ones posting the gender reveal images. You feel your heart is going to explode with excitement. What is all *this* about?

Maybe you went from being a rock star at work to being a stay-at-home parent. Your identity has been shaken to its core. What is all *this* about?

Or maybe being a stay-at-home parent has been the thing your soul needed. What is all *this* about?

Maybe you're retired and spend your days and money on doctor's appointments instead of the travel you always dreamed of. What is all *this* about?

Or maybe you're wondering why you didn't figure out how to retire sooner. Your marriage has never been so fun.

Finances up, finances down, moments of laughter, moments of tension, sex life great, sex life not so much, in-laws helping, in-laws hurting, ups, downs, what...is...all...*this*...about?

What is the purpose of all *this*?

What is the purpose of marriage?

It's a good question to ask, and I think married people should have the answer to this question nailed. Knowing the purpose of anything we do of substance is huge. If you are building a house and things get delayed, you keep going because you know there is a bigger purpose. If you are running a company and go through economic challenges, you work to figure it out because there is a bigger purpose. If your car breaks down on vacation, you get it fixed and keep going because there is a bigger purpose.

I believe knowing the purpose of marriage is a huge deal—especially if you are interested in having a *great* marriage. **Knowing the purpose of marriage not only helps you get through the tough stuff, it helps you to enjoy the great stuff.** Unfortunately, most married people don't know the purpose of marriage—or at least a purpose important enough—to fuel them during the confusing highs and lows.

So, what is the purpose of marriage? Turns out there are several. One purpose of marriage is companionship. We all have legitimate emotional and relational needs; marriage seems like a long-term solution for that. And doesn't God say in Genesis that it is not good for a man to be alone? Yup. (Although my wife likes to point out that God doesn't say, "It is not good for a woman to be alone". She enjoys her "me time" very much.) What about having children? Isn't that one of the purposes of marriage? Sure, for some, but not all.

The Big One

But as important as companionship and procreation might be, I think there is an even greater purpose for marriage that we forget, don't know, or confuse. And knowing this purpose of marriage is massively important to our Us.

Now, you may be thinking, if knowing the purpose of marriage is so important, then why did you save it to the end of the book? That's a great question. There are a few reasons I saved it for last. For starters, you may have some push backs to the answer. Or you may think the answer doesn't apply to you. Or it may seem too lofty, poetic, ethereal, or hyper-spiritual. Or—and this is a biggie—it may seem unfair. **And while knowing this purpose of marriage may cause the most push-backs *in you,* it may also have the most potential *for you.***

Knowing the purpose of marriage just may motivate you to handle a 30-year-old issue in a new way. It may help you enjoy the little things more. It may be the thing that makes the question "what is *this* about?" have more meaning. It may free your heart to love better and be better loved. But primarily, I saved the main purpose of marriage until now, because I do believe in saving the best for last. I think understanding this purpose does a great job of summing up the whole point of this book by giving you one more intentional thought to tie the other intentional thoughts together.

I believe the most compelling purpose of marriage comes from Ephesians 5. Ephesians 5 was a letter written by the Apostle Paul to new followers of Jesus in the city of Ephesus. Given the content of the letter, it appears people haven't changed much in the last 2000 years. If this letter showed up in your mailbox today, I promise you, it couldn't be more relevant, practical, and profound. About 2,500 words in, Paul offers instructions for married people. I can't help but think about the first hearers of these words. I'm certain these married people also asked themselves, what is all *this* about? Then come the words that not only answer the question about the purpose of marriage, but also answer how to live out that purpose. Are you ready? Paul writes in Ephesians 5:21

> *Submit to one another...*

So, how do those four words hit you? I imagine the same way they hit the first listeners—and me, "Oh no! Boo! Submit to one another? What about that is sexy or fun? Submit to one another? Does that mean what I think it does, that I put my spouse's needs ahead of my own?"

The short answer (and also the long answer) is: Yes.

Our Knee-Jerk Reaction

It's not sexy or fun. In fact, it can feel nearly impossible because self-sacrificing is not our natural tendency. Our natural tendency is the exact opposite: to look out for ourselves FIRST. Occasionally we see this play out here in my great home state of Georgia. (Yes, I've changed my opinion of Georgia since moving here.) When my fellow Georgians and I spot even one single snow flurry coming from the sky, our initial instinct is to rush out to buy bread, eggs, and milk. IMMEDIATELY. Because French toast is the best thing the French didn't invent, and people might have a hankering to make French toast in the impending snowpocolypse. I get it. We have to eat, and purchasing perishable items we don't normally eat because everyone else does, makes total sense. Sort of. But this is our default behavior. We all have in us the tendency to race to the front of the line to get ours. We want to be first, at the top, in the front. And self-sacrificing is the exact opposite of that.

A Better Option

Pastor Andy Stanley says, submitting to one another in marriage is like two people racing to the back of the line. This type of marriage is two people saying to one another, “You go first,” “No you go first,” “No you”, “No you.” This type of marriage requires us to decide that we will, *“love first.”* The thought of this type of approach to marriage may seem nearly impossible—for all of us.

I'm as guilty of this as the next person. Our natural tendency to want to have our needs and wants met first, is why submission is so difficult. Submission is not natural. It requires humility. And our default mode of thinking in marriage is usually not “submit to one another”. Instead, we can tend to think, “They don't meet *my* needs. Why should I meet *theirs*?”

It's easy to spend time and mental energy convincing ourselves—and even others—how poorly we are treated by our spouse. We do this because our level of submission to our spouse is often based on our spouse's level of submission to us. How well we love them is often based on how well they are loving us. Some of us are meticulous score-keepers. But mutual submission doesn't keep score. It doesn't constantly scan the relationship ensuring what is fair. In other words, mutual submission is terrible at math and couldn't care less about balancing the equation. Self-sacrificing is a completely different way of thinking that asks no less than all we have to give. It can feel nearly impossible. But when it's practiced? When your marriage is made up of two people racing to the back of the line? It's beautiful. When you live it, it's stunning.

I realize this may already be causing some fears and frustrations in you, many of which may be completely valid. But before I address them, I'd love for you to dream with me for a bit.

Who's “That” Couple?

A mutual submission marriage is a beautiful thing to behold. And part of what makes it so beautiful is how practical it is. *“Love first”* spouses get up and make the coffee. *“Love first”* spouses unload the dishwasher when they see the clean light is on. (Full disclosure: I hate that example because I would rather build a log cabin than unload the dishwasher. But that is a *“love first”* move at my house.) A *“love first”* spouse has conversations with their spouse when they prefer watching Netflix. I've just pushed things too far, haven't I? Perhaps that's not fair, but it is beautiful.

With that in mind, when you think about a couple who puts their spouses' needs ahead of their own, what couple do you think of?

I think of my family. I watched my stepmom care for my dad's mother. No one would have expected her to, my dad didn't ask her to, and everyone would have understood if she hadn't. But she did and it was a stunning picture of submission. My dad also helped take care of my stepmom's late husband's parents. It wasn't expected or fair and my stepmom didn't ask him to, but it was a brilliant picture of submission. After my aunt who helped raise me died, my uncle remarried several years later. His new wife hosts Christmas for our family. That's right, she hosts Christmas for her husband's late wife's family. It wasn't expected or fair, my uncle didn't ask her to, but it is an exquisite picture of submission.

My friend Casey, in the middle of a successful music career, said to his wife, whose interior design career was taking off, "I will step back from my music and stay home with our four little girls. I want you to have the time to focus on what you are passionate about." It wasn't expected or fair, but it was a brilliant picture of submission.

Tom and Crystal, after several years and multiple rounds of reproductive procedures, got pregnant with their daughter, Everly. Everly was born 20 weeks too early, and only lived for what Tom and Crystal describe as 19 glorious days. Their loss was not fair. I do not understand it and I am sure I never will. Yet, no one can deny the beauty of how Tom and Crystal have clung to, supported, and submitted to each other. Their selfless-love for one another has been one of the most beautiful things I've ever had the privilege to see.

But That's Not Fair

Despite the brilliance and beauty of submission, it evades many of us. As much as we know it is best, right, and the most loving thing to do for the person we love most, sometimes we just won't do it. And perhaps the thought that stops us from loving that way the most is the line:

"But that's not fair!"

Unfortunately this line isn't just popular in our marriages. It's a common refrain among children. It seems we just haven't managed to mature beyond this childish instinct. The apostle Paul addresses this in his letter to the church in Corinth when he writes, *When I was a child, I talked like a child, I thought like a child, I reasoned like a child. When I became a man, I put the ways of childhood behind me (1 Corinthians 13:11 NIV).*

Turns out, our inclination to be childish isn't a new thing. But that doesn't mean we need to stay stuck in that way of living. Submission to our spouse requires us to grow up a bit—for the good of our spouse, ourselves, and our Us.

Is Submission Worth It?

From unloading dishwashers to being there for your spouse during unspeakable pain, mutual submission is a beautiful picture of heaven on earth. Like your favorite athlete, piece of art, or landscape, it's impossible to describe *why* mutual submission is so beautiful. We just know it is. The closest word I can find to describe it is luminous.

Luminous is defined as: *full of or shedding light; bright or shining, especially in the dark.*

This type of love in marriage shines brightly in the dark. And I don't need to tell you, in a world full of so much darkness, light is something we could stand to have more of. This type of relationship is a light.

So, what is the purpose of marriage this type of loving and living leads to? What is the point of your marriage? What is the purpose of your Us? This next part of the verse shows us. Drum roll and marching band, please....

> *Submit to one another out of reverence for Christ (Ephesians 5:21 NIV).*

The purpose of marriage is to reflect the love of Jesus.

If you aren't a follower of Jesus, that purpose may not resonate with you. But make no mistake about it, the first part of that verse is just great advice for anyone. Putting your spouse's needs ahead of your own offers great hope for any marriage, no matter your faith or beliefs.

But if you are a follower of Jesus, I hope this purpose hits your heart in a fresh yet permanent way. I pray this purpose matters to you because of what you have experienced from Jesus Himself. Jesus modeled the way for us to love each other in our marriage and when we do this well, we have more than a great marriage, we highlight the character of God.

Driving Aunt Sue

The most beautiful version of a "love first" marriage I ever saw was my great Aunt Sue and Uncle Bob. Their entire marriage they put each other first, so when Aunt Sue was diagnosed with Alzheimer's Disease, no one was surprised to see Uncle Bob serve her day in and day out. But the degree to which he did it was a thing to behold. Alzheimer's caused Aunt Sue to be very restless and she eventually became nonverbal. She always seemed to be looking for or fussing with something. She just couldn't seem to get settled, with one exception: when Bob was driving her around in the car.

I had heard of the rides Bob and Sue had taken together, but had no idea of their scope until the day of her funeral. That's when we learned that Bob had driven Sue to all 48 states in the continental U.S. After the funeral, he casually mentioned they were headed to Alaska but turned back because it made him a little nervous. *Alaska*? Uncle Bob was not a young man, but had been caring for Aunt Sue in every possible way. Of course it was difficult. Of course it wasn't fair. But it was beautiful because it was a "love first" kind of love.

A Beautiful Bridge

No one is confused by or has pushbacks with this type of "love first" kind of love. Whether you're into Jesus or not, when you see "love first" love modeled, you can't help but stare. Regardless of how you feel about Christianity, witnessing a self-giving love like Jesus', lived out in real life, is captivating. Because the truth is, you don't have to love Jesus to want your marriage to work. If you are married, you want your marriage to win. Period. But the beauty of it is, a marriage that is winning is also shining a light on the kind of love God demonstrates and has for us. It's the best kind of love that can't help but draw the attention and wonder of a watching world.

God chose marriage to be that light to the world and a bridge to the kind of love God demonstrates. And it doesn't take a perfect marriage to be that, but a couple that lives with a "love first" Jesus kind of love. In other words, married people who love Jesus are a well-constructed, well-lit bridge to Jesus and the church. I love that image.

The Big One

And *that's* what the purpose of marriage is. To show what the best kind of love, a self-giving love, looks like, so that people can better witness, and then demonstrate that same kind of Jesus love to others. **The purpose of marriage is to reflect the love of Jesus.** That is your purpose, that is the point of *all this*.

It makes sense. In Jesus' life and death we see exactly what self-giving love looks like. There is no longer any question of what God is like and what love is like. Jesus demonstrated it. He made the way. And now, Jesus invites us to participate in it with Him. He invites us to love sacrificially. And something that beautiful can't help but draw us to it and demand a response. Even sitting here right now, as I write, the thought of what Jesus has done to demonstrate His love is more than I can grasp—in the best possible way.

Remembering Is Key

Even so, I can easily forget and get caught up thinking about what is fair for *me*. I can make the dishwasher more important than modeling after Jesus. I can make winning an argument more important than being kind. These small things—and so many of them really are small—serve as a constant reminder of the incredible lengths Jesus was willing to go, to demonstrate the kind of love He has for us. His life and death show us His love in the big and small ways. And when we consider the tenderness He has for us, we can't help but be wowed by the fact, He could, He would, love us like He does.

Nancie reminded me of this in a recent text. She sent me a link to a song from Patrick Mayberry entitled, "How You Love Me." Her text read "This one is going to wreck you." She was right. It continues to wreck me. Patrick sings, *"Could it really be this easy, that You love me like You say you do? Could it really be this simple? Your kindness changes everything. You're not mad and you're not scary, and all this shame and guilt I've carried is why you died for me. Hallelujah. All this time. How You love me."*

Could it really be this simple? That He loves you like He says he does? Is it true that His kindness changes everything? What if God isn't mad or scary? What if all this shame and guilt you've carried is why He died for you— Hallelujah. All this time. How He loves you.

I don't know where you are with Jesus. Maybe the idea of seeing Jesus this way makes you uncomfortable. Maybe you have never thought of Jesus in such a personal or intimate way. That's okay. I just want you to know that the God of the universe is willing to go to any length possible to demonstrate affection towards you.

In the same way, I don't know where you are in your marriage. Maybe the idea of a "love first" marriage feels impossible. Maybe that seemed possible at one time, but things feel so far gone that recovery is a pipe dream. I get it. But I also know that radical self-giving for the good of another person can change hearts, change lives, and change marriages. When we love like Jesus did, anything is possible.

I know it's not easy to demonstrate that kind of love. I know it's easy for us to forget the kind of love Jesus has for us. I know it's easy to make excuses and treat our spouse in the way we think they deserve. And the truth is, it is terrifying to live in a self-giving way, because putting our spouse's needs ahead of our own may make us vulnerable. We think if we aren't looking out for ourselves who will? But fear and a desire to protect your own ego will keep you from loving in this radical way—in a way that could change your marriage but will most definitely change you.

Self-giving love is life giving love.

Wait a Minute

That being said, loving self-sacrificially never means putting yourself in harm's way. It doesn't mean allowing your spouse to hit you, berate, or hurt you in any way. That is not self-sacrificial love. That is abuse. God doesn't want that for you, your children, or anyone. But unfortunately, people have mistreated this passage of urging submission to trap people in marriages that were unsafe and the exact opposite of a representation of what God's love is like.

Hold On

On the other hand, we can't treat divorce like an escape hatch. One man recently told me he knew he needed to divorce, but he just couldn't seem to do it. His small group from church and his parents had told him to divorce, but he said for some reason he just couldn't. He seemed to be calling me to convince him they were right. But, when he shared his story, there didn't seem to be any cause for divorce—no abuse of any kind, no infidelity on either side.

All the advice he received was based on him protecting himself in case his wife was preparing to "take everything he had." It was based on their opinions that she was being unreasonable. Everything he was doing in response to their advice, was pushing her further and further away. All the advice she was receiving was leading her to do things that were pushing him further and further away. On both sides, the advice they were being given was based on the philosophies of self-protection and fairness.

I share that to say, not all advice is created equal. Chances are, we know the people who will tell us exactly what we want to hear. And we know who the people are who challenge us and cause us to think more critically about our behavior and thought patterns. So, when it comes to any advice, choose your advisors wisely. Don't just go to people who will tell you what you want to hear. Go after the advice and the advisors who will reinforce the purpose of marriage.

So where are you getting your advice and information about marriage? Friends, family, the Internet? What and who are your echo chambers?

Check your sources to ensure you are making decisions based on God's purpose for marriage: reflecting the love of Jesus. Find people who are for you *and* for your marriage—people who are willing to tell you the difficult truth about yourself that may be hard to hear—especially if talk of divorce is on the table. Because for most of us, our worst moments are not worthy of an exit. In fact, your worst moments can serve to start the reconstruction process of building back to being better than ever. Something happens when we support each other during tough times.

Plus, there is something motivating about realizing our marriages are bigger than us, that there is something we are aiming for that is beyond us. And when we realize there is something better for our spouse and our marriage on the other side of this difficulty, it can give us the push we need to see a better reality beyond it. More than that, we owe it to ourselves, our spouse, and others affected by our marriage, to see what happens when we live life putting our spouse's needs ahead of our own.

How Will They Know?

Jesus said, *"By this everyone will know that you are My disciples, if you love one another" (John 13:35 NIV).* For married people, there is no other *"one another"* more important than your spouse. That's the point of taking the time to love well. That's the point of being intentional with your thoughts. The point of all this, the point of our Us, is to reflect the love of Jesus. You are to serve as a light, a bridge to who God is for your kids, your family, your friends, your co-workers, your community, and your world. In fact, every one of the **intentional thoughts** included in this book, were written with that purpose in mind. When you:

— *remember who you are,* you will love more like Jesus.
— *see the best,* you will love more like Jesus.
— *choose empathy,* you will love more like Jesus.
— *pause,* you will love more like Jesus.

And perhaps nothing can help you reflect the love of Jesus more than the next and final intentional thought...

INTENTIONAL THOUGHT #5

⇨ "Love first."

During moments when you think, "I just can't do this"—and in every marriage, those moments will come—think to yourself and even say out loud if you can, *"Love first."* Saying to yourself "Love first" frees your mind to love like Jesus in a self-giving way, even when it is difficult. I can't make any promises your spouse might not keep, but there is no greater hope for your marriage than to love following the model Jesus gave us.

Think About It

Reflecting the love of Jesus is the point of marriage. That is why, for the next 30 days, I want you to say out loud to yourself twice a day—once in the morning and once before you go to bed—the following

Five Intentional Thoughts. . .

I will...

○ Remember who I am.

○ See the best.

○ Choose empathy.

○ Pause.

○ Love first.

There's a reason why repeating these phrases is part of the plan to make a better marriage a reality. Recent studies revealed that simply repeating a phrase twice a day can have a radical impact on your life. Jon Acuff in his book, *Soundtracks,*[19] had people say out loud to themselves in the mirror twice a day, what he called, A New Anthem. The New Anthem consists of a brief introduction statement and 10 statements, including things like:

1. "Today is brand-new and tomorrow is too."

2. "I've got a gift worth giving."

3. "The only person standing in my way is me, and I quit doing that yesterday."

The purpose was to help people accomplish their goals by getting them to stop what Jon calls, over-thinking. He defines **overthinking as, when what you think gets in the way of what you want.** After 30 days, he was blown away with the results. After repeating positive affirmations twice a day for 30 days, people were 250% more likely to decrease their over-thinking, worked an average of nine more days a month on their goals, and raised success rates for goals by 21%.

The point is this. What you say to yourself matters because your thoughts ultimately influence your actions. Because of that, I think you will find becoming more intentional with your thoughts about your marriage for 30 days will make a difference. Your thoughts will start impacting your behavior. And if these thoughts still seem impossible to implement and pointless in the realm of your marriage, I want you to be encouraged. God has a much larger view of you and your marriage than just the current moment you are in. That means we can trust how God has invited us to live, as difficult as it may seem to be. God's ways of thinking come from a higher perspective than ours. I love how that fact is communicated in The Message translation of Isaiah 55:8-11:

"I don't think the way you think.
The way you work isn't the way I work.
For as the sky soars high above earth,
so the way I work surpasses the way you work,
and the way I think is beyond the way you think.
Just as rain and snow descend from the skies
and don't go back until they've watered the earth,
Doing their work of making things grow and blossom,
producing seed for farmers and food for the hungry,
So will the words that come out of my mouth
not come back empty-handed.
They'll do the work I sent them to do,
they'll complete the assignment I gave them."

For me, knowing God's thoughts are higher than mine is oddly reassuring. I don't get a lot of what has happened to me in my life. I don't understand why I was born with a brain that is challenged by ADHD and anxiety. I don't understand why I've experienced so much loss and grief. I also don't understand why I have all the things I love about my life and family. I don't understand why I have the privilege to encourage you in this book. I don't understand why some spouses are great and other spouses aren't. I don't understand why some people can have babies and others can't. I don't understand why finances, communication, and sex are so easily and joyfully experienced by some and not by others. I don't understand LOTS of things. But I'm comforted that I can trust who God is and that means I can take seriously how God instructs us to love one another. We can trust and be intentional about repeating these thoughts:

1. Remember who I am
2. See the best.
3. Choose empathy.
4. Pause.
5. Love first.

These are not necessarily our natural thoughts, but they could be the way to save, transform, protect, and enrich your marriage. Becoming more intentional with your thoughts could radically alter your future and the future of those you care about. While I can't make any guarantees, I must still ask you: what do you have to lose? Why *not* try it? If nothing else changes, *you* will. And that's no small thing.

Chapter Seven

What Do You Think Is Possible?

I WANT TO END OUR TIME TOGETHER BY SHARING specifically how these five intentional thoughts have impacted my life and marriage in hopes it will give you encouragement for yours. As I told a friend of mine recently, while I still have a long way to go—we all do—the content of this book is changing my life. I pray with my whole heart that it changes yours too. And speaking of prayers, I want to close by praying for you too. Can you pray for someone in a book? Sure you can.

Intentional Thought #1: Remember Who You Are

My daughter recently asked me, "Dad, are you okay?" I said, "Yes, why?" to which she answered: "You are just being quiet." The very next day Nancie asked me the same question, "Are you okay?" I said, "Yes, why?" And she said, "You are just quieter than usual."

Do you want to hear something weird? (Of course you do.) In both those scenarios, I really *was* okay. My really perceptive daughter and wife were just *off* on how they interpreted my behavior. I was feeling good. In fact, I've never been better. Why? Because I've never *thought* better.

The intentional thoughts from this book have revolutionized my own mind and, by extension, my marriage. I don't say that to give myself a pat on the back. I share that to give you hope. Like I said earlier in the book, if I can do what I've presented on these pages, anyone can.

Fred in my head has been my unwelcome companion since I was a child. But now I know how to better handle him and that has mattered greatly to me and my marriage. I am more settled, at peace. To my family that has come across as quieter—and they may be right. These days I sing around the house less than I did when Fred was in charge. Let me explain. My entire family is used to me singing *a lot*. All of my kids have always had their own theme songs that I have sung to them since they were babies. I've also—don't judge me—unintentionally taught them more 80's and 90's TV theme song lyrics than Scripture. When we are in the car and I have to quickly change lanes, I sing the theme song from the A-Team and when I get a song stuck in my head, everyone around me is going to know. But no one is more affected by my love of song singing than Nancie. She, by far, has the most songs sung about her. I can quickly turn ANY song into a song about her, simply by replacing a lyric with her name or nickname—the Pug. So yes, my entire family can tell you that I am an incessant singer. And regardless of whether they see this as adorable, maddening, or somewhere in between, it has been a part of me, a part of my family, and a part of our Us. So it was confusing to my family, and even me, why I started singing less.

But then it hit me. While I sing my kids' theme songs and Nancie's love songs out of love and affection, a lot of my singing has been about blocking *out* Fred's voice. So now that I can hear God's voice more clearly without the incessant loud lies from Fred, I am quieter. I can be quiet, I actually don't *have* to sing. Because there's peace. Silence is no longer scary. Now when I do sing, it's from a joyful place, not a "Fred, would you shut your piehole" place.

I've also been able to slow down more lately... just a bit. I believe I'm a busy person by nature and design. My life is full with Nancie, our four kids, friends, family, work, household fix-its, and chores, and of course, work. My job requires me to travel quite a bit, sometimes even flying to two cities in one weekend to speak. But recently, I've caught myself being calmer in the middle of it all. While the things I do in my life are not different, I do them differently. I can listen more intently. I can *almost* sit still. I am becoming more naturally responsive versus reactive. I've even caught myself enjoying my backyard and not just maintaining it. I'm sleeping better. I...prepare yourself for a cliche...can be more present. I feel better and I love better because I think better. For that I'm so grateful.

Much of my frantic pace has been to shut Fred out, shut him up, prove him wrong. In other words, much of my life has been impacted by Fred in one way or another. So learning to know I am loved, and then living like I'm loved, has quieted my soul in the best way. Fred is no longer the driver of my story. So when even those who know and love me best ask, "Are you okay?" More often than not, I can say, "Yes, better than ever." I want that for you too, I want you to have more peace than ever. This is my prayer for you:

> *God, You know and love the person who holds this book. Would You do that thing only You can do, where You whisper into their hearts how much You love them? Would You quiet their Freds? Would You maybe even make their Freds shut up so they can hear You whisper how much You love them? Would You turn this moment into a miracle where they start to know who they are—someone radically loved by You?*
>
> ***God, I pray the reader of these words in this moment, will start to hear Your voice as the loudest voice in their heads.***

Intentional Thought #2: See the Best

As I mentioned earlier, I struggled with seeing the best in Nancie during a certain season of our marriage. My own pain made me selfish. But now I would say "see the best" has become the easiest of all the five intentional thoughts—probably because I've had so much time to retrain my brain to see the best. I learned about the research on the power of seeing the best in your spouse about fifteen years ago. I was so personally impacted by what I learned, I almost immediately started writing and speaking on the topic. And I've been yapping about the Philippians 4:8 filter ever since.

In all fairness, "see the best" should be the easiest for me. Nancie is so easy to think well of. But I realize that is not the case for many people. After recently hearing me teach this content at a marriage retreat, Nancie said, "I think this stuff is easier for us because we really like each other." She went on, saying, "I think for the person who is in a marriage where they really don't like their spouse, this must be much harder to hear." Point taken, and I couldn't agree more.

I've worked with enough couples to know, dealing with a very difficult spouse isn't easy. But while seeing the best can feel impossible, it is so worth it! And the Philippians 4:8 filter we talked about earlier, really does help you see the best. It positions and postures you to love in a way that is healing to you and, maybe even more, healing to your spouse. There is a peace and hope that comes with knowing you are doing all *you* can. There is a peace and hope that comes with knowing that whatever comes of the relationship, you did all you could do to love well. My prayer for you:

> *God, if the person reading this book is hurting because they are dealing with a spouse who is really difficult, I pray You hold them in this moment. If they are unsafe, I pray You would provide them with distance and wisdom. For the person who just needs to have an honest conversation, I pray it is couched in what comes from seeing the best of their spouse. If their issues stem from the small annoyances, I pray You would help them to focus on what they do love about their spouse instead. God, I pray what they love about their spouse will block the view of what they don't.* ***I pray most of all that they would see their spouse the way You do.***

Intentional Thought #3: Choose Empathy

While "see the best" is the easiest of the intentional thoughts for me, "choose empathy" remains the most challenging. But when I made the intentional decision to work at getting better at this, the effect was almost immediate. I mentioned this earlier, but it bears repeating. When I simply say, "That's understandable," I'm blown away at how effective AND easy it is. And not just for me, for Nancie too. Nancie will admit that she, like her husband, is a fixer. If I am Bob the Builder, she is Wendy. Can she fix it? Yes, she can! (If you don't know who Bob and Wendy are, don't learn, it's better that you don't. Trust me.) Also, having her say to me more and more, "That's understandable," or "That's fair" has been an accelerant to getting Fred out of my head. A "that's understandable" from Nancie, helps me to trust myself and God more and Fred less. Together, we are both learning that when we are searching for advice, we will specifically ask the other for it. All the other times *should* be reserved for empathy. Full stop.

But that's not all empathy has done. Empathy has helped me celebrate how different Nancie and I are. Empathy forces me to see things from her perspective, to walk a mile in her shoes. And when I do? I almost always find her shoes are ill-fitting and not my style—which is the point. **Empathy turns *flaws* into differences.** For instance, I'm a dreamer, she's a realist. It used to frustrate me that she didn't like to dream about potential home projects. I'm pretty handy, and typically have some sort of home improvement project going. I used to say to her, "You don't have to help me do the project, but I do need you to dream about them with me." But she quite simply doesn't enjoy dreaming about home projects. She says talking about home projects doesn't bring her joy, it brings her stress. That is not a flaw, that is a difference. She said, "You always do a great job with things around the house. I trust whatever you decide." So, instead of trying to change or guilt her into becoming a dreamer, I can enjoy the fact she trusts me to dream and implement things on my own. **What used to be a point of contention, is now a point of connection.** But that couldn't have happened without a mindset shift towards empathy. My prayer for you:

> *God, thank You for softening my tough heart and head when it comes to empathy. I pray You would soften the heart and head of the person reading these words in this moment. I pray You would bring to mind where they need to be more empathetic with their spouse. Help them to see through their frustration to see what is real and important to their person.*

God, I pray You would help them to see their spouse, get their spouse, and let their spouse know, "I got you!"

Intentional Thought #4: Pause

I was five-years-old, standing in front of the one-hundred-person congregation of Fairview United Methodist Church. Each Easter, every child would give a short Easter speech or poem, and I was ready to give mine. But my mom, evidently, did not think I was ready to give mine. She was sitting in the front row and when I started my speech, she started mouthing the words to me. I calmly stopped my speech and said to her, "Stop doing that. I want to do it all by myself." I started over, but when I was just a few lines back into my speech, she started mouthing the words again. This obviously triggered my amygdala, because I, to use a southern phrase, "pitched a fit." I started crying and stomping my feet and my mom tried to "retrieve" me, but I outran her. Then my Sunday School teacher tried to catch me, but I easily juked her. BUT there was no juking my dad. He scooped me up, and quickly took me out of the church. As you can imagine, I was never able to live this down. How could I? An entire church body, especially my family, refused to let me. And in all fairness, I can't blame them. It was quite a show.

Apparently, I came into this world a very passionate, independent person. This spirit in me, this wiring, is part of why I'm able to stand in front of audiences and encourage them today. But it is also the part of me that has led to the most embarrassing and regrettable moments of my life and marriage. Based on my experiences, may I say to you—especially if you are quick-to-the-draw when it comes to your emotions—*there is a better way.* I've learned a better way. And this better way has led to a better life with fewer regrets. In fact, I can tell you from my own life, that **a better term for controlled emotions is regret management.** Because when you and I pause, it is a superpower.

The same little reactionary guy that pitched a fit in front of the entire church, who punched kids on the playground, who got angry with teachers, who struggled as a teenager, who made poor choices in college, who said things in ministry and relationships he shouldn't, who said things to his wife and kids that he shouldn't, has learned a new way. Am I perfect at it? Of course not. But I can confidently say, I have learned a new way, and if I can, I am sure you can too. My prayer for you:

God, when we are calm, in our best moments, we know that quick reactions are wildly inferior to thoughtful responses. For the person reading these words, would You help them to learn how to pause long enough to love well? Would You help them to wait long enough to be the spouse You know they can be?

God, I pray You would help the person reading this prayer to be quick to listen to their spouse, slow to speak to their spouse, and slow to become angry with their spouse.

Intentional Thought #5: Love First

Talking about the purpose of marriage in the previous chapter was tough. I love being able to give really simple applications to people who live in a really complicated world. Practical application can feel more boots on the ground, while purpose can appear to be more about flying at 30,000 feet. But despite its lofty nature, **marital purpose informs and lives in the most mundane of moments.** This specific truth reveals itself to me time and time again as my wife and I co-parent, co-chore, and co-exist. There are multiple times every day, when I get the opportunity to love first.

As I'm finishing this book, I've been face to face with love first opportunities. This week my daughter is going to day camp. The drop-off and pick-up is an hour each way. My sweet wife, knowing I'm on a deadline, offered to do the two hours of extra driving all week. Part of me thought, "You should just let Nancie do it. You have so much on you this week." But "love first" said, "No, that's too much for Nancie to do alone. Take your daughter every morning." This week gave me another "love first" opportunity last night. The book cover options have left me feeling torn to the point of losing sleep. So my head has been buried in my computer more than normal. One night after dinner Nancie looked at me and said, "Would you put your computer away and talk to me?" Part of me thought, "She should understand how much stress you are under and how much this means to you. You don't normally do this." "Love first" said simply, "Shut your computer and be with your wife."

You get it. Marriage gives you countless opportunities to love first. This opportunity for you may be in the area of finances, or in-laws, or communication, or sex, or toilet paper. Whatever it is, the area where it is the most challenging to be self-sacrificing, is the area where it has the most impact. So as you think about where you need to love first, start with the place where it is the hardest. That may sound like counterintuitive advice. But if you can put your spouse first in this area, everything else will feel easier in comparison. My prayer for you:

> *God, the person reading this book needs Your energy to love first when it's not fair. You promise that You refresh those who refresh others. I pray they will experience the refreshment that comes from loving first. And when they do, I pray others would see that You are the reason they love the way they love.*
>
> ***God, I pray the person reading this prayer in this moment will be nothing less than inspired to love the way You love.***

Imagine

God has done some amazing things in me since I've become more intentional with my thoughts. I want you to have what God has uniquely for you too. So much so, it has even made the process of writing this book worth it. And friends, as I write the final words, I will say to you, the process has not been easy. After all, I am still...me. But the thought of **you** keeping your Us in mind, changing your marriage by changing your thoughts, has been the thing that has kept me going. You are worth every trip to the library, every edit. You are even worth the misery of making sure the citations are punctuated correctly! You are EVEN worth every wrestling match with Fred!

Why? Because I imagine you finding freedom from your Fred. Because I imagine you **seeing** the amazing things that have always been true of your spouse. Because I imagine you **looking** at your spouse in a way that lets them know you are there. Because I imagine you **responding** more and reacting less to your spouse. Because I imagine you **loving** first in big and small ways.

Now I want you to imagine for yourself—

1. What would it look like for me to challenge the thoughts in my head about myself?

2. What would it look like for me to share with my spouse all the great things I see in them?

3. What would it look like for me to stop trying to fix my spouse and just be there for them?

4. What would it look like for me to simply pause the next time I get frustrated or angry?

5. What would it look like for me to love first even when I think it's not fair?

Imagine. Imagine if these **five intentional thoughts** became a regular part of your thinking process.

- Remember who I am.
- See the best.
- Choose empathy.
- Pause.
- Love first.

No really, imagine if you took this seriously. Imagine what the people closest to you might observe between you and your spouse. As difficult as it might seem to make these changes, wouldn't it be worth it? For you, for your spouse, for your US? It would be worth it, because you are, your spouse is, your marriage and the people it impacts, are worth it. I really do believe it. And my prayer is that not only do you believe it, but that you begin to live and love like you know this to be true.

Notes

1 Buckingham, M. (2006). *The One Thing You Need to Know: About Great Managing, Great Leading, and Sustained Individual Success*. Pocket Books.

2 Fisher, H., & big think. (2016, February 13). *The Science of Love, with Dr. Helen Fisher | bigthink*. YouTube. Retrieved June 27, 2022, from https://www.youtube.com/watch?v=0YP4n9G0qtQ

3 Dweck, C. S. (2016). *Mindset: The New Psychology of Success*. Ballantine Books.

4 Shapiro, L., & Long, H. (2018, August 8). *Analysis | Where Do You Fit In The Global Income Spectrum?* The Washington Post. Retrieved July 25, 2022, from https://www.washingtonpost.com/graphics/2018/business/global-income-calculator/

5 Heath, C., & Heath, D. (2013). *Decisive*. Crown Business

6 Brown, B. (2021, March 21). *Hello Monday with Jessi Hempel: Brené Brown on getting it right on Apple podcasts. Apple Podcasts*. Retrieved August 15, 2022, from https://podcasts.apple.com/us/podcast/bren%C3%A9-brown-on-getting-it-right/id1453893304?i=1000513892989

7 Baisden, D. W., & Her View From Home. (2022, January 4). *Stop being a Butthole wife*. Her View From Home. Retrieved June 27, 2022, from https://herviewfromhome.com/stop-being-a-butthole-wife/

8 Zach Brittle, L. M. H. C. (2017, August 9). *E is for empathy*. The Gottman Institute. Retrieved June 27, 2022, from https://www.gottman.com/blog/e-is-for-empathy/

9 Bloom , L. & C. (n.d.). *Why You and Your Partner Need to Celebrate Each Other*. Psychology Today. Retrieved June 27, 2022, from https://www.psychologytoday.com/us/blog/stronger-the-broken-places/201609/why-you-and-your-partner-need-celebrate-each-other

10 Okura, L. (2017, December 7). *The Most Vulnerable Emotion We Experience*. HuffPost. Retrieved June 27, 2022, from https://www.huffpost.com/entry/brene-brown-joy-numbing-oprah_n_4116520

11 Lowe, T. (2016). *Your Best Us: Marriage is Easier Than You Think.* Orange.

12 Stosny, S. P. (2009). *How to Improve Your Marriage Without Talking About It.* Crown Publishing Group.

13 Jung, N., Wranke, C., Hamburger, K., & Knauff, M. (2014, June 10). *How Emotions Affect Logical Reasoning*. Frontiers in psychology. Retrieved June 28, 2022, from https://www.ncbi.nlm.nih.gov/pmc/articles/PMC4050437/

14 Crabtree, S. (2021, March 31). *Mirror Neurons.* Happy Brain Science. Retrieved June 28, 2022, from https://www.happybrainscience.com/blog/mirror-neurons/

15 Zach Brittle, L. M. H. C. (2022, May 9). *Turn Towards Instead of Away.* The Gottman Institute. Retrieved June 27, 2022, from https://www.gottman.com/blog/turn-toward-instead-of-away/

16 Zach Brittle, L. M. H. C. (2018, October 26). *R is for Repair.* The Gottman Institute. Retrieved June 27, 2022, from https://www.gottman.com/blog/r-is-for-repair/

17 Evans, V. (2020, January 23). *How Does Communication Work?* Psychology Today. Retrieved June 27, 2022, from https://www.psychologytoday.com/us/blog/language-in-the-mind/202001/how-does-communication-work-0

18 Brown, B. (n.d.) *Brené Brown's Rule When She's Feeling Shame: Don't talk, Text, or Type*. Podclilps. Retrieved June 27, 2022 from https://podclips.com/c/vDFtCM?ss=r&ss2=brene brown&d=2022-05-04

19 Acuff, J. (2021). Soundtracks: *The Surprising Solution to Overthinking.* Baker Books, a division of Baker Publishing Group.

Appendix

Psalm 139:13-15 ESV
For you formed my inward parts; you knitted me together in my mother's womb. I praise you, for I am fearfully and wonderfully made. Wonderful are your works; my soul knows it very well. My frame was not hidden from you, when I was being made in secret, intricately woven in the depths of the earth.

Jeremiah 29:11 ESV
For I know the plans I have for you, declares the Lord, plans for welfare and not for evil, to give you a future and a hope.

Luke 12:6-7 ESV
"Are not five sparrows sold for two pennies? And not one of them is forgotten before God. Why, even the hairs of your head are all numbered. Fear not; you are of more value than many sparrows."

1 Corinthians 10:13 ESV
No temptation has overtaken you that is not common to man. God is faithful, and he will not let you be tempted beyond your ability, but with the temptation he will also provide the way of escape, that you may be able to endure it.

Romans 12:2 ESV
Do not be conformed to this world, but be transformed by the renewal of your mind, that by testing you may discern what is the will of God, what is good and acceptable and perfect.

Colossians 3:12-14 ESV
Put on then, as God's chosen ones, holy and beloved, compassionate hearts, kindness, humility, meekness, and patience, bearing with one another and, if one has a complaint against another, forgiving each other; as the Lord has forgiven you, so you also must forgive. And above all these put on love, which binds everything together in perfect harmony.

Titus 3:5 ESV
He saved us, not because of works done by us in righteousness, but according to his own mercy, by the washing of regeneration and renewal of the Holy Spirit,

Romans 5:8 ESV
But God shows his love for us in that while we were still sinners, Christ died for us.

Philippians 4:8-9 ESV
Finally, brothers, whatever is true, whatever is honorable, whatever is just, whatever is pure, whatever is lovely, whatever is commendable, if there is any excellence, if there is anything worthy of praise, think about these things. What you have learned and received and heard and seen in me—practice these things, and the God of peace will be with you.

Matthew 11:28-30 ESV
"Come to me, all who labor and are heavy laden, and I will give you rest. Take my yoke upon you, and learn from me, for I am gentle and lowly in heart, and you will find rest for your souls. For my yoke is easy, and my burden is light."

Proverbs 28:6 ESV
Better is a poor man who walks in his integrity than a rich man who is crooked in his ways.

Romans 12:3 ESV
For by the grace given to me I say to everyone among you not to think of himself more highly than he ought to think, but to think with sober judgment, each according to the measure of faith that God has assigned.

Psalm 139:14 ESV
I praise you, for I am fearfully and wonderfully made. Wonderful are your works; my soul knows it very well.

James 4:6 ESV
But he gives more grace. Therefore it says, "God opposes the proud, but gives grace to the humble."

1 John 4:19-21 ESV
We love because he first loved us. If anyone says, "I love God," and hates his brother, he is a liar; for he who does not love his brother whom he has

seen cannot love God whom he has not seen. And this commandment we have from him: whoever loves God must also love his brother.

1 Samuel 16:7 ESV
But the Lord said to Samuel, "Do not look on his appearance or on the height of his stature, because I have rejected him. For the Lord sees not as man sees: man looks on the outward appearance, but the Lord looks on the heart."

Ephesians 2:10 ESV
For we are his workmanship, created in Christ Jesus for good works, which God prepared beforehand, that we should walk in them.

John 16:33 ESV
"I have said these things to you, that in me you may have peace. In the world you will have tribulation. But take heart; I have overcome the world."

Matthew 16:26 ESV
"For what will it profit a man if he gains the whole world and forfeits his soul? Or what shall a man give in return for his soul?"

Ephesians 4:32 ESV
Be kind to one another, tenderhearted, forgiving one another, as God in Christ forgave you.

Romans 3:23 ESV
For all have sinned and fall short of the glory of God,

John 3:16 ESV
For God so loved the world, that he gave his only Son, that whoever believes in him should not perish but have eternal life.

Philippians 4:13 ESV
I can do all things through him who strengthens me.

Philippians 2:2-8 ESV
Complete my joy by being of the same mind, having the same love, being in full accord and of one mind. Do nothing from rivalry or conceit, but in humility count others more significant than yourselves. Let each of you look not only to his own interests, but also to the interests of others. Have this mind among yourselves, which is yours in Christ Jesus, who,

though he was in the form of God, did not count equality with God a thing to be grasped, ...

Genesis 1:27 ESV
So God created man in his own image, in the image of God he created him; male and female he created them.

2 Timothy 1:7 ESV
For God gave us a spirit not of fear but of power and love and self-control.

Luke 18:9–14 ESV
He also told this parable to some who trusted in themselves that they were righteous, and treated others with contempt: "Two men went up into the temple to pray, one a Pharisee and the other a tax collector. The Pharisee, standing by himself, prayed thus: 'God, I thank you that I am not like other men, extortioners, unjust, adulterers, or even like this tax collector. I fast twice a week; I give tithes of all that I get.' But the tax collector, standing far off, would not even lift up his eyes to heaven, but beat his breast, saying, 'God, be merciful to me, a sinner!' ...

Isaiah 41:10 ESV
Fear not, for I am with you; be not dismayed, for I am your God; I will strengthen you, I will help you, I will uphold you with my righteous right hand.

2 Corinthians 5:17 ESV
Therefore, if anyone is in Christ, he is a new creation. The old has passed away; behold, the new has come.

Matthew 10:29–31 ESV
"Are not two sparrows sold for a penny? And not one of them will fall to the ground apart from your Father. But even the hairs of your head are all numbered. Fear not, therefore; you are of more value than many sparrows."

1 Peter 2:9 ESV
But you are a chosen race, a royal priesthood, a holy nation, a people for his own possession, that you may proclaim the excellencies of him who called you out of darkness into his marvelous light.

Mark 12:31 ESV
"The second is this: 'You shall love your neighbor as yourself.' There is no other commandment greater than these."

Matthew 5:5-9 ESV
"Blessed are the meek, for they shall inherit the earth. Blessed are those who hunger and thirst for righteousness, for they shall be satisfied. Blessed are the merciful, for they shall receive mercy. Blessed are the pure in heart, for they shall see God. Blessed are the peacemakers, for they shall be called sons of God."

Matthew 7:7 ESV
"Ask, and it will be given to you; seek, and you will find; knock, and it will be opened to you."

Isaiah 58:10-11 ESV
If you pour yourself out for the hungry and satisfy the desire of the afflicted, then shall your light rise in the darkness and your gloom be as the noonday. And the Lord will guide you continually and satisfy your desire in scorched places and make your bones strong; and you shall be like a watered garden, like a spring of water, whose waters do not fail.

Psalm 139:13 ESV
For you formed my inward parts; you knitted me together in my mother's womb.

Joshua 1:9 ESV
"Have I not commanded you? Be strong and courageous. Do not be frightened, and do not be dismayed, for the Lord your God is with you wherever you go."

Song of Solomon 4:7 ESV
"You are altogether beautiful, my love; there is no flaw in you."

Philippians 1:6 ESV
And I am sure of this, that he who began a good work in you will bring it to completion at the day of Jesus Christ.

Zephaniah 3:17 ESV
The Lord your God is in your midst, a mighty one who will save; he will rejoice over you with gladness; he will quiet you by his love; he will exult over you with loud singing.

Proverbs 15:1 ESV
A soft answer turns away wrath, but a harsh word stirs up anger.

Hebrews 4:16 ESV
Let us then with confidence draw near to the throne of grace, that we may receive mercy and find grace to help in time of need.

Ephesians 1:4 ESV
Even as he chose us in him before the foundation of the world, that we should be holy and blameless before him. In love

Proverbs 3:5-6 ESV
Trust in the Lord with all your heart, and do not lean on your own understanding. In all your ways acknowledge him, and he will make straight your paths.

Jeremiah 31:3 ESV
The Lord appeared to him from far away. I have loved you with an everlasting love; therefore I have continued my faithfulness to you.

Luke 12:7 ESV
"Why, even the hairs of your head are all numbered. Fear not; you are of more value than many sparrows."

Matthew 9:10-13 ESV
And as Jesus reclined at table in the house, behold, many tax collectors and sinners came and were reclining with Jesus and his disciples. And when the Pharisees saw this, they said to his disciples, "Why does your teacher eat with tax collectors and sinners?" But when he heard it, he said, "Those who are well have no need of a physician, but those who are sick. Go and learn what this means, 'I desire mercy, and not sacrifice.' For I came not to call the righteous, but sinners."

Isaiah 43:4 ESV
Because you are precious in my eyes, and honored, and I love you, I give men in return for you, peoples in exchange for your life.

1 Peter 3:3-4 ESV
Do not let your adorning be external—the braiding of hair and the putting on of gold jewelry, or the clothing you wear— but let your adorning be the hidden person of the heart with the imperishable beauty of a gentle and quiet spirit, which in God's sight is very precious.

Colossians 3:1 ESV
If then you have been raised with Christ, seek the things that are above, where Christ is, seated at the right hand of God.

Ephesians 1:5-6 ESV
He predestined us for adoption as sons through Jesus Christ, according to the purpose of his will, to the praise of his glorious grace, with which he has blessed us in the Beloved.

1 Peter 3:4 ESV
But let your adorning be the hidden person of the heart with the imperishable beauty of a gentle and quiet spirit, which in God's sight is very precious.

Ephesians 4:1-6 ESV
I therefore, a prisoner for the Lord, urge you to walk in a manner worthy of the calling to which you have been called, with all humility and gentleness, with patience, bearing with one another in love, eager to maintain the unity of the Spirit in the bond of peace. There is one body and one Spirit—just as you were called to the one hope that belongs to your call—one Lord, one faith, one baptism, ...

John 3:17 ESV
"For God did not send his Son into the world to condemn the world, but in order that the world might be saved through him."

John 1:12 ESV
But to all who did receive him, who believed in his name, he gave the right to become children of God,

Psalm 100:3 ESV
Know that the Lord, he is God! It is he who made us, and we are his; we are his people, and the sheep of his pasture.

James 1:22-27 ESV
But be doers of the word, and not hearers only, deceiving yourselves. For if anyone is a hearer of the word and not a doer, he is like a man who looks intently at his natural face in a mirror. For he looks at himself and goes away and at once forgets what he was like. But the one who looks into the perfect law, the law of liberty, and perseveres, being no hearer who forgets but a doer who acts, he will be blessed in his doing. If

anyone thinks he is religious and does not bridle his tongue but deceives his heart, this person's religion is worthless.

Philippians 2:3 ESV
Do nothing from rivalry or conceit, but in humility count others more significant than yourselves.

Proverbs 31:30 ESV
Charm is deceitful, and beauty is vain, but a woman who fears the Lord is to be praised.

1 John 3:16 ESV
By this we know love, that he laid down his life for us, and we ought to lay down our lives for the brothers.

James 4:11-12 ESV
Do not speak evil against one another, brothers. The one who speaks against a brother or judges his brother, speaks evil against the law and judges the law. But if you judge the law, you are not a doer of the law but a judge. There is only one lawgiver and judge, he who is able to save and to destroy. But who are you to judge your neighbor?

Psalm 27:10 ESV
For my father and my mother have forsaken me, but the Lord will take me in.

Ephesians 4:31-32 ESV
Let all bitterness and wrath and anger and clamor and slander be put away from you, along with all malice. Be kind to one another, tender-hearted, forgiving one another, as God in Christ forgave you.

2 Corinthians 3:18 ESV
And we all, with unveiled face, beholding the glory of the Lord, are being transformed into the same image from one degree of glory to another. For this comes from the Lord who is the Spirit.

Matthew 7:1-5 ESV
"Judge not, that you be not judged. For with the judgment you pronounce you will be judged, and with the measure you use it will be measured to you. Why do you see the speck that is in your brother's eye, but do not notice the log that is in your own eye? Or how can you say to your brother, 'Let me take the speck out of your eye,' when there is the log in

your own eye? You hypocrite, first take the log out of your own eye, and then you will see clearly to take the speck out of your brother's eye."

Proverbs 3:1-35 ESV
My son, do not forget my teaching, but let your heart keep my commandments, for length of days and years of life and peace they will add to you. Let not steadfast love and faithfulness forsake you; bind them around your neck; write them on the tablet of your heart. So you will find favor and good success in the sight of God and man. Trust in the Lord with all your heart, and do not lean on your own understanding.

Matthew 26:41 ESV
"Watch and pray that you may not enter into temptation. The spirit indeed is willing, but the flesh is weak."

Proverbs 25:28 ESV
A man without self-control is like a city broken into and left without walls.

Galatians 2:20 ESV
I have been crucified with Christ. It is no longer I who live, but Christ who lives in me. And the life I now live in the flesh I live by faith in the Son of God, who loved me and gave himself for me.

John 14:6 ESV
Jesus said to him, "I am the way, and the truth, and the life. No one comes to the Father except through me."

Jeremiah 1:5 ESV
"Before I formed you in the womb I knew you, and before you were born I consecrated you; I appointed you a prophet to the nations."

1 John 4:4 ESV
Little children, you are from God and have overcome them, for he who is in you is greater than he who is in the world.

Philippians 3:13-14 ESV
Brothers, I do not consider that I have made it my own. But one thing I do: forgetting what lies behind and straining forward to what lies ahead, I press on toward the goal for the prize of the upward call of God in Christ Jesus.

Matthew 16:24-25 ESV
Then Jesus told his disciples, "If anyone would come after me, let him deny himself and take up his cross and follow me. For whoever would save his life will lose it, but whoever loses his life for my sake will find it."

Isaiah 49:15 ESV
"Can a woman forget her nursing child, that she should have no compassion on the son of her womb? Even these may forget, yet I will not forget you."

2 Corinthians 12:9-10 ESV
But he said to me, "My grace is sufficient for you, for my power is made perfect in weakness." Therefore I will boast all the more gladly of my weaknesses, so that the power of Christ may rest upon me. For the sake of Christ, then, I am content with weaknesses, insults, hardships, persecutions, and calamities. For when I am weak, then I am strong.

Matthew 6:31-34 ESV
"Therefore do not be anxious, saying, 'What shall we eat?' or 'What shall we drink?' or 'What shall we wear?' For the Gentiles seek after all these things, and your heavenly Father knows that you need them all. But seek first the kingdom of God and his righteousness, and all these things will be added to you. Therefore do not be anxious about tomorrow, for tomorrow will be anxious for itself. Sufficient for the day is its own trouble."

Proverbs 19:11 ESV
Good sense makes one slow to anger, and it is his glory to overlook an offense.

Mark 12:30 ESV
"And you shall love the Lord your God with all your heart and with all your soul and with all your mind and with all your strength."

James 4:1 ESV
What causes quarrels and what causes fights among you? Is it not this, that your passions are at war within you?

Romans 12:1 ESV
I appeal to you therefore, brothers, by the mercies of God, to present your bodies as a living sacrifice, holy and acceptable to God, which is your spiritual worship.

Proverbs 3:5 ESV
Trust in the Lord with all your heart, and do not lean on your own understanding.

1 Corinthians 6:20 ESV
For you were bought with a price. So glorify God in your body.

Isaiah 43:1 ESV
But now thus says the Lord, he who created you, O Jacob, he who formed you, O Israel: "Fear not, for I have redeemed you; I have called you by name, you are mine.

John 3:16-17 ESV
"For God so loved the world, that he gave his only Son, that whoever believes in him should not perish but have eternal life. For God did not send his Son into the world to condemn the world, but in order that the world might be saved through him."